HOUSE OF RETREAT, PLESHEY

By kind permission of the Warden

LIGHT OF CHRIST

Addresses given at the House of Retreat
Pleshey, in May, 1932

by

EVELYN UNDERHILL

Hon. D.D., Aberdeen
Fellow of King's College, London

With a Memoir by Lucy Menzies

Wipf & Stock
PUBLISHERS
Eugene, Oregon

Wipf and Stock Publishers
199 West 8th Avenue, Suite 3
Eugene, Oregon 97401

Light of Christ
Addresses given at the House of Retreat Pleshey, in May, 1932
By Underhill, Evelyn
Copyright©1945 Wilkinson, R.D.
ISBN: 1-59244-646-9
Publication date 4/8/2004
Previously published by Longmans, Green and Co., 1945

CONTENTS

FRONTISPIECE
HOUSE OF RETREAT, PLESHEY

EVELYN UNDERHILL

*A life sufficiently large to take up and retain within
its own experimental range, at least some of the poignant
question and conflict, as well as of the peace-bringing
solution and calm; hence a life dramatic with a humble
and homely heroism which in rightful contact with and
in rightful renunciation of the Particular and Fleeting,
ever seeks and finds the Omnipresent and Eternal; and
which again deepens and incarnates (for its own experience and apprehension and for the stimulation of other
souls) this Transcendence in its own thus gradually
purified Particular: only such a life can be largely
persuasive, at least for us Westerners and in our times.*

FRIEDRICH VON HÜGEL.

WHEN the manuscript of this book came into my
hands it seemed to me as I deciphered it day by
day that it gave a picture of Evelyn Underhill as
her friends knew her; that here she described what
she fain would be, what indeed as far as human nature
may be, she was. In a way undreamt of by herself
these meditations reveal her inner life. She wrote
them in the spring of 1932 when she was busy as usual
with another book. When, having heard them at
Pleshey in May of that year, I asked her whether she
would not· publish them then, she replied, "Not
now!" implying that they might appear later. We
believe that they do now appear with her approval
although they were not revised for the printer by
herself. They are the fruit of long thought and meditation. They were written, altered, amended in a

9

notebook which went everywhere with her. I remember, for instance having lunch with her in the shelter of a friendly haystack during a long drive north; the note-book came out of her bag and was studied and written in. Its contents therefore grew out of her daily life and practice.

These meditations represent the spoken rather than the written word. She had, like her teacher, Baron von Hügel, a way of driving home her teaching by an unconventional expression or a homely example. There was never anything formal or stereotyped about her or the Retreats she gave.[1] They were full of life, of zest, of humour. What she said often pierced to the heart as when, after allowing some particularly devastating remark to sink home, she would say quietly, looking up, "How do we feel about *that*?" She identified herself with her flock. She was showing them a path along which she herself was travelling, and all the discoveries as to the best way she put generously at their disposal.

Although she wrote books which opened windows into the Unseen to many, she would have agreed that her chief work in her latter years was the giving of Retreats and the "after-care" of those—and many others!—with whom she thus came in contact. Because I happened to be Warden at Pleshey during the years in which she gave most of her Retreats there, I have been asked to put down a few reminiscences for her friends.

Making a Retreat with Evelyn Underhill was a serious matter. Yet when told once that the experience had been a "shattering" one, she replied that it ought not to have been so; since the ideal she put

---

[1] For the benefit of those not conversant with Retreats, a paper in which Evelyn Underhill explains what a Retreat is and what it tries to do is reprinted on p. 102.

before her hearers was a counsel of perfection, an ideal to be striven after rather than attained in this world. That she tried to live according to her own teaching no one who knew her can have any doubt; how far she achieved it, those who knew her best will realize.

Although she gave retreats elsewhere—at Moreton, St. Leonards, Canterbury, Leiston Abbey, Watermillock, Glastonbury, and so on, Pleshey was the first Retreat House she knew and from the first she loved it. There was a natural attraction between her and that plot of ground on the outskirts of Pleshey village now called the House of Retreat. It used to be known in the neighbourhood as " The Holy Land," for a Religious House had stood on it since the fourteenth century, and although swept away by the Reformation, it was later revived by a contemplative community. Froissart's *Chronicle* tells us that in 1393, Thomas, Duke of Gloucester, Regent of England, "being in great danger by reason of a tempest at sea, vowed solemnly that if he escaped he would erect a College to the honour of the Holy Trinity." He did escape and he and his wife, Eleanor de Bohun, one of the richest heiresses of England, built and endowed a College of "nine chaplains, two clerks and two choristers," a foundation upon which they lavished rich gifts, lands and manors, tapestries, vestments (there were as many as 58 copes!), jewelled vessels, illuminated missals, etc. Although the actual buildings have disappeared, the intention of the pious founders in establishing a house where the spiritual life could be lived and spiritual ideals fostered is carried on by the House of Retreat. The Community of the Servants of Christ built the present House as a Convent for themselves in 1907 and though they outgrew their foundation, their prayer still supports it. The ground it stands on is holy ground from which prayer has gone up as incense for hundreds of years. Prayer is its life. Its whole atmosphere invites to communion with God.

It is easy to understand how the beauty of holiness found at Pleshey delighted Evelyn Underhill. She loved the wide expanse of sky and the great fields of that open Essex country; she loved too the Pleshey garden, its moat and its moorhens, its freedom and its joy in the Lord. She wrote to a friend:

"I loved Pleshey this time and indeed it was more like having a Retreat than giving one. They were such a splendid set and the flavour seemed turned on all the while. I had nothing to do but swim along. On Sunday morning before the 10 o'clock Address it was very wonderful—a living silence filled the Chapel. I daren't go on for a bit. . . .

"All the country round was wrapped in a lovely hazy golden russet. I thought of you listening for the little threefold bell[1] and could feel you and the Baron and Mrs. Rose with your dynamos turned on and helping."

Pleshey never felt more alive than when she and her flock were there. They worked hard, they prayed hard and the whole place—steeped as it is in centuries of prayer and adoration—was full of Life and Light. Everything down to the smallest detail was thought

[1] Many things about the House of Retreat are meant to sustain and foster the traditions of Pleshey College. The bell rung before each service rings three times three strokes to symbolize the dedication of College and Chapel to the Holy Trinity.

of and arranged beforehand, so that the whole mind and heart and soul of all present might be fixed wholly upon God. E. U. would be found in the porch of the Chapel soon after she arrived, putting up all particulars—suggestions for Bible readings, Points for Meditation, times for interviews, the Hymn Sheet, etc. (She was very particular about hymns, which were carefully chosen for each Address—and woe betide the organist if the hymns dragged!) She always claimed at Pleshey the privilege of acting as sacristan and especially of preparing the Altar for the Eucharist.

Latterly there was often a verse of some poem pinned up in the porch as a key-note, sometimes written out in script by herself (an art she practised as a relaxation). One year there was this verse of Donne:

"Since I am coming to that Holy Room
  Where with the choir of saints for evermore
  I shall be made Thy music—as I come
  I tune the instrument here at the door,
  And what I must do then, think here before."

She often illustrated her Addresses by reference to some great picture, a reproduction of which she would put up in the porch. And once finding a letter from the Abbé de Tourville[1] to someone about to make a Retreat which completely agreed with her own conception of what a Retreat should be, she put that also in the porch and urged her hearers to lay it to heart. Just because it so entirely expressed her own views, it is quoted in full:

What you have to do in your Retreat is very simple: namely to make it with great simplicity.

[1] From *Piété Confiante*

Such faults, weaknesses, failures, lassitude, lack of goodwill and so forth, as you see in yourself, are not to cause you fear and anxiety, but rather humility and confidence. You are simply to say, 'Yes! I am like that, yet all this will not prevent God from making something of me in spite of myself and indeed of making me a thousand times more sanctified than, left to myself, I should ever have thought possible.' This is humility and confidence.

Thus everything in your Retreat which reawakens self-reproach for those faults of which we are full, which suggest fear of failing in your response to God, you will transform into this joyful humility and unshakable confidence. All that is consoling and encouraging you will accept without reserve, remembering the unspeakable generosity of God who delights to overwhelm even the sinful and evil soul with gifts, especially when it lifts up its hands towards Him.

Avoid all strain and effort, try to be quiet and passive, dealing with your impressions in this way as they arise. Breathe in the grace of God as we breathe in the air, with tranquillity, without effort or self-consciousness. By this deliberate calm and quietude, maintained throughout your Retreat, you will gain more than you can conceive. I speak of that which I know.

You will say, 'But then I shall have made no special preparation and the days will go by with no special result!'

I reply, 'The Lord will have entered more peacefully and more fully into the soul which is more simple and less over-strained, less worried, less tense. The result of your Retreat, while less consciously felt, will be more lasting and more solid. The great result will be that you will begin to perceive the prevenient and invincible lovingkindness of God. That is the fathomless ocean into which you must enter, never to find yourself again.'

HENRI DE TOURVILLE.

If one were asked to say in one word what was the heart of Evelyn Underhill's teaching, it would surely be—GOD. Adoration was for her *the* essential. When that had been practised there was not much time for anything else, certainly not for self. As Richard of St. Victor points out, "The desirous soul no longer thirsts *for* God but *into* God. The pull of its desire draws it into the Infinite Sea." Yet there is much labouring at the oars to be done before the Ocean Pacific of the Godhead is reached. It cannot be drifted into, least of all by such as Evelyn Underhill. "Storms come down on us without warning," she writes, "and drive us off our course." Here the great Augustinian saying naturally delighted one who knew the sea so well, *I toss upon the waves but Thou dost steer Thou Who standest at the helm of all things Thou hast made.* She had an illumination of that saying on her desk and its implication was very present to her.

She not only had "the sea and Europe" behind her, as Charles Williams points out;[1] she also had mountains. She writes in this book, "I remember once in the Alps finding myself alone in a high pasture surrounded by the strange almost unearthly mountain life. I was filled then with that absolute contentment and solemn happiness which hardly anything else can give to those who have the mountain

[1] *Letters*, p. 7.

sense." The present writer remembers being with her once in Norway, high up on a mountain pasture on a golden summer afternoon, a small summit still within reach. She was tired but the summit called her and she sped eagerly away to it.

She tells us in these addresses that a Retreat ought to be something like an experience of the mountains —"a pause when we can look across the valley and see the great spiritual snowfields in their beauty." Her Retreats were in fact something like that—"a convicting and purifying message of holiness and sacrifice and love." When she writes of the Father's business being the only business of man "and not very spectacular" at that, she is unwittingly describing her own life. "Ordinary life, love, devotedness," she says, "will do very well for the revealing action of God." Beyond that, however, she was one in whom something "Other" was found by all sorts and conditions of men. And to a rare degree. That explains why so many went to her for help. She was so easy to talk to, so natural, there was no alarming hint of the scholar and writer. She was very simple in her life, even in some ways to the verge of austerity. When owing to her health that became foolish, she acquiesced in care and comfort, only occasionally confessing "how beastly" it was.

Her life was unspectacular, but it was very full. What really saved her was the fact that she belonged to a legal family and partook of the spacious legal holidays of those times. But she arrived at those holidays drained to the last drop of her vitality.

She wrote her own books, reviewed other people's books for various papers, edited the texts of the mystics, was for a time religious editor of the *Spectator*, visited her poorer neighbours in North Kensington, saw people who needed her help in the afternoons and gave four or five Retreats every year—not to mention all the lectures she was asked to give and papers she was asked to read, activities from which she did her best to withdraw as her own real work became more and more pressing. Her correspondence was formidable. Yet she loved her letters; she was very faithful about answering them and had the gift of doing so in any free moment, in the train, on the yacht, sitting in a field or at her own fireside.

Although her life in London was very happy—her home, her work, her friends—she was devoted to the country and escaped to it whenever possible. She writes from Stony Cross on arriving one Whitsun Eve:

"Here we are in a little tiny Hotel all by itself on the forest edge—adorable wild ponies feeding all round it, with lots of foals. Off the roads the whole country is like a morass, but green and lovely and the trees in greatest splendour. We have been rambling gently about all day and getting such splendid views over miles of woodland and heaths. The yellow flags and orchis and pale blue marsh forget-me-not are all out and a certain amount of hawthorn left too. Yesterday we had tea at Fordingbridge on the edge of the Avon which is in flood. You would have been interested in a water-rat which sat on the bank just below us, very nice and furry and cleaned its face with its paws. . . ."

Holidays, "rambling gently along" in this way, were spent visiting all parts of Britain. She had an intimate knowledge of the ecclesiastical architecture of this country and of Italy and France as well.

B

Birds and flowers of the countries visited were also known to her with the delight of the field-naturalist. And of course there was the sea which she had known and sailed from her youth up. Even if we did not know that, we would infer it from her easy use of nautical terms. They really meant something to one who not only sailed her own boat but (in Father Talbot's vigorous phrase) always "held the boat of her soul up into the wind."

She had great delight, too, in her garden where in summer she used to write surrounded by such plants as would consent to grow in the London atmosphere. Once having consented, they grew with a will and did in fact produce a green profusion among which meals could be enjoyed in summer, the traffic of that Western Road which had inspired one of her early poems, streaming out, a dim accompaniment in the background.

Such were the factors which counteracted the strain under which she lived. Not that her personality suggested strain, rather a deep tranquillity. She had on her study mantelpiece a small oblong panel with the word ETERNITY worked on it; it drove home the conviction of those privileged to penetrate to that book-lined room, that there one stood within the frontiers of Eternity. Because, for all her creatureliness she never left the mystery out. One was very conscious of that in her company. "It is not Christian to leave the mystery out," she writes; "Christ does not leave it out; His teaching has a deep note of awe, a solemn sense of God and the profound mystery of God. . . . His teaching all ends in one thing, GOD, who is greater than our heart. Once we have learnt that lesson, all else falls into place."

So it seemed to her friends, everything fell into

place in her; they saw in her the cherishing, merciful action she described, the compassion reaching out, the gay, spendthrift giving of health and strength, and it revealed to them "the untiring loving-kindness that dwells in the heart of Reality." Words she wrote about Baron von Hügel, her final court of appeal in all things spiritual, come naturally to mind in thinking of his disciple, for they might have been written about herself:

"Solid, simple, sober souls were the type he most approved, and sought to form. The 'mystical element' of religion was never allowed to dominate the field, or become the one basis of faith. Our poor little human experience of Reality, he taught, must always fluctuate. . . . But 'God and Christ and the need of our constant death to self remain *simply certain*.' Hence self-abandonment was the crowning virtue and 'humbling and bracing' were the twin qualities he looked for in spiritual reading and prayer. . . .

"Secular interest and employments took a prominent place in his conception of the ordered spiritual life. . . . Moreover, such an ordered life invariably included some care for and, if possible, direct intercourse with the poor . . . 'God, Christ and the poor' is a trilogy that occurs frequently in his private correspondence as does the steady insistence on every form and degree of homely love: 'I deeply love my little dog and the Abbé Huvelin was devoted to his cat. We can and will become all the dearer to God for this our 'love of our little relations, the smaller children of God.'"[1]

1 *Mixed Pasture*, pp. 231, 232.

Having sat at the feet of the Baron for many years it was not surprising that she drank deeply of his spirit. But even before they met, they had had much in common in great things as in small. She had begun work among the poor very early and she kept that up as long as her health allowed. Another thing she and the Baron had in common was the saving grace of humour, that characteristic of the saints. She too constantly brought the homely and the sublime together—this doubleness, this capacity for moving easily between the homely and the transcendental, the natural and supernatural levels runs right through her life, conversation and teaching too, sometimes appearing with disconcerting effect.

She was really humble or rather, in her own phrase, "self-emptied." To someone foolish enough to praise her vocation, "what a wonderful work she was doing for God!" she exclaimed brusquely, "*Only* trying to be a decent third housemaid!" It must be allowed that she did not suffer fools gladly—bores even less—but she did her best about it and achieved a patience which must have been difficult to her vehement nature.

Her spirit enabled her for years to keep her asthma at bay. As soon as an attack was over pencil and paper would somehow mysteriously be in her hands and she would get on with her job (or a note to an anxious friend—"No one knows I am writing this!"). She would even get out of bed and drive down to Pleshey for a heavy week-end of addresses and interviews; she writes of one such effort:

"I had the nearest possible shave of not getting to Pleshey as I was suddenly laid low by 'flu the previous week-end . . . I was in bed till Thursday but by firm, steady prayer and determination, got up on Friday *perfectly well* and remained and still remain so—shouldn't have known I'd had an illness! It is really rather startling—I feel like a Lourdes *miraculée*. Dr. very puzzled and thought it was bluff—but not at all. No cough, no asthma. . . . And I had plenty to do as I had to say Compline as well as all the rest. . . .

"Mrs. Harvey[1] was as dear as ever and let me prepare the Altar each day."

The point is that the work she had come to do was done through her, and although she looked so fragile and transparent that one feared a breath might really blow her away, yet she conveyed to many the strength to move their mountains. She was well content to pay the price.

It is not only in her scholarship, her writings, her genius for life and friendship—for she was a great friend—that we find the real E. U. but in her instant response to the need of any with whom she came in contact. All these she felt to be her "job." She really practised Ruysbroeck's "wide-spreading love to all in common." Clever or stupid, spiritually advanced or unconverted, members of any Church or of none, wherever she saw need she gave instant response. She hints at the cost when she says, "The call of those who need us is apt to take us away from what we love to do." She met all such calls gladly because she cared so much. "Caring matters most" was a favourite saying of the Baron's. Evelyn Underhill lived it. And that made those who sought her help feel at home. She took a deep interest even in the little things of their lives, their hobbies, their

[1] First Warden of Pleshey.

animal friends, their amusements, all of which she felt to be important; and she lent her books with "spendthrift" generosity (one of her favourite and very characteristic words!). Her flock was very near her heart, constantly in her thoughts and prayers; any special job, any difficult bit of work would have its send-off from her in a letter of encouragement— "God will be with you!"

And she in her turn counted on the help her friends could give her. Every spring she sent out a little typed slip with the dates of her Retreats for the year; her friends were asked to put it in their Prayer Books and to pray for each Retreat as it came. One wondered sometimes at the heights to which she led her flock, the serener air they breathed, the sense of power which sustained them. But when on the last evening she read out the names of those who had been remembering the Retreat, part of the secret was revealed. The little company had been "hedged around" with prayer.

She believed in prayer and self-giving which are indeed, or which were at least in her, the same thing. That was the secret of her life and it is summed up by St. John of the Cross:

Absolute self-giving is the only path from the human to the Divine.

LUCY MENZIES

"SHINE into our hearts, O loving Master, by the pure light of the knowledge of Thyself, and open the eyes of our minds to Thy teaching; that in all things we may both think and act according to Thy good pleasure and meditating on those things that are holy, may continually live in Thy Light."

Dawn Office, Eastern Church.

I

PREPARATION

A GREAT many of us are here to-night for the first time so I hope those who have been often before will bear it if we think a little about what a Retreat ought to be. It is a period in which we withdraw from the restless surface of life in order to give our whole attention to the deeps of life: cut off relations with our visible environment which generally obsesses us, in order to realize better, if we can, our invisible environment—GOD—and adjust ourselves better to Him, His demands, His gifts. The silence is there, of course, to help that adjustment by cutting off one of the most obvious of all distractions. "Blessed" said Thomas à Kempis, "be the ears that heed not outward speech but hear the whisper of God." For this above all else we make a Retreat whatever else we put into it and whatever form it takes—to hear the whisper and see the light that comes to us from beyond the world and shows us how to live. We all wish to be taught how to live, don't we? and to go on being taught how to live, and the longer we go on with life, the more mysterious it seems to us and the more deeply we feel that need. We go muddling on, knowing we are making a hash of it; people tell us this and that, but somehow they all seem rather like guesses in the dark, and they all fail to be any real use when we come to the bad bits. And at last we realize that only the Author of human life can really teach us to live human life. He alone knows what it is meant to be. And the only way to

25

lay hold of this secret, or to recapture it, is to come
to God and be alone with Him.

Thou hast the words of Eternal Life. We come into
the silence to hear those words again and true ourselves up to that which they say. So a time like this
can be a very rich experience if taken the right way.
Yet even so, God Himself cannot explain to us our
true life as He sees it in its reality, any more than
we can explain its true life to the cat. He sees each
one of us in relation to His Eternity, sees us as little
things He is making for Himself. *He* sees us within
a spiritual world and surrounded and conditioned by
spiritual forces of which *we* know hardly anything at
all, but which are infinitely more important and more
powerful than all the things we fancy matter a great
deal. We are much like children in the nursery, much
concerned with all our toys, meals, etc., but never
thinking about home routine, about heat and electric
light, still less of the human ideal for which nursery
life is the preparation. Nevertheless God can come
to His human children and show our life to us as it
ought to be: show it to us in our terms, not His; try
to make us see what it can be if nothing happens to
spoil His perfect work of art. His Word—*Logos*—
His Christ, can be made flesh and dwell among us. *In
the beginning was the Word*—the Word, the self-
expression of Reality—and the Word came to us in
Christ our Master, not as an explanation of life but
as a direction how to live it, and a very homely,
arduous direction too—"God" as Hebrews has it
"speaks in a Son."

So we have added something else to the object of
our Retreat: it is a time when we can listen to the
secret whisper of the Spirit and look at Christ again,
for the contemplation of Christ is the first part of

Christianity. One will help the other, enrich the
other. The doctrine of the Trinity means that many-
sided revelation of God and expression of God.

A time like this can be such a rich experience if we
take it the right way—open up our souls, open our
spiritual ears and eyes' to the "beauty of the Mystery." Don't let us waste all the time merely exam-
ining our own state! If we look steadily and humbly
at Christ's life and see in it the truth about human
life and especially our own lives as His servants and
fellow-workers, each time we look we shall find ourselves shrinking by contrast and at last we shall be
so small we shall become as little children. Nothing
could be better than that!

Contemplation of Christ does not mean an emotional sort of pious day-dream; it means entering by
a deliberate, self-oblivious and humble attention into
the tremendous mysteries of His Life—mysteries
which each give us some deep truth about the Life
and Will of God and the power and vocation of a
soul that is given to God—mysteries which each one
of us in particular is called to make part of our very
lives. They will break up, into colours we can deal
with, that white light of God's Holiness at which
we cannot look.

You know sometimes how one goes to see a church
which one is told has magnificent windows— and seen
from outside they all look alike—dull, thick, grubby.
We probably say, "Well! it is obvious there is good
glass here but we cannot realize it." Then we open
the door and go inside—leave the outer world, enter
the inner world—and the universal light floods
through the windows and bathes us in their colour
and beauty and significance, shows us things of which
we had never dreamed, a loveliness that lies beyond

the fringe of speech. And so in the same way we cannot realize God and all our Lord's lovely meaning as a revelation of God and His eternal Truth and Beauty, from outside. One constantly hears people commenting on Christianity from outside and missing the point every time. They are on the wrong side of the wall. How important then it is for us to be familiar with the inner vision. It is from within the place of prayer, recollection, worship and love, where the altar is, where the sacrifice is made, where we are all bound together in a life of communion and self-giving to God, that we fully and truly receive the revelation which is made through Christ. Then we see the different acts and stages of His life like a series of windows through which streams into our souls the pure light of God, mediated to us in a way we can bear: Eternity and Reality given to us in human terms. To re-enter that Cathedral, receive a fresh gift from its inexhaustible beauty, see through those windows more and more of the light of God, that is the secret of meditation. Julian says at the end of her *Revelations* that what she had received from her vision of Christ was "Light, Life and Love"; everything was gathered in that; an energy to show us the Truth, quicken us to fresh vitality and fill us with adoring devotion. What a contrast to our stodgy, vague, twilit inner life! We come into the silence to get more Light, Life and Love. We come to contemplate our Christian treasure from inside.

Some of us perhaps remember the experience of standing for the first time inside Chartres Cathedral; the solemn, coloured majesty that enfolds us and silences us when we come into the place of adoration and sacrifice; and how gradually we become aware of the strangeness of the light that strikes us through those great coloured windows. A Retreat can be such an experience of God's glory, filling the whole universe. But the absolute Light only dazzles us; in its wholeness it is more than we can bear. It needs breaking-up before our small hearts can deal with it. The windows of Christ's Mysteries split it up into many-coloured loveliness, disclose all its hidden richness and colour, make its beauty more accessible to us; convince us of the reality of beauty and holiness and of the messy unreality of most of our own lives. And within this place we too are bathed in the light transmitted by the windows, a light which is yet the very radiance of Eternity. It fills the place where we are, it drowns us in its solemn beauty and glows in the Figure and acts which we see. The universal light of the Father, the interior radiance of the Holy Spirit, linked together in this vision of the Son, so far above us and yet so divinely near.

Now I want our Retreat to be like that: to dwell in the silence, and let the light from the windows penetrate, purify and quicken our souls, enhance our sense of truth and beauty, our self-abandoning love.

First of all we look east and we see over the altar a vision of Christ triumphant ruling the whole creation—the perfect victory of God's thought and love. And then we look round at the method and cost of that triumph. What we see is not very sensational but if we look steadily it pierces the heart. First we see a baby and a long, hidden growth and the gradual outpouring and self-spending of an other worldly love and mercy in teaching, in healing, rescuing and transforming, but never trying to get anything for itself; in a mysterious self-imparting and a more mysterious anguish and struggle; at last we see the most lonely and generous of deaths, giving life ever since to men's souls. There they are: not just finished works of art or memorials of past beauty, but always mediating the Spirit, setting up a standard for us and quivering with the living Light and Love. *I am He that lived and died and am alive for ever more.*

You know how Plato spoke of this life as a cave in which men were imprisoned and could only judge reality by seeing the shadow cast by light outside. But for Christians the cave has become a great shrine in which we are taught and moulded for the purpose of our creation—a sacrificial life in union with God. We come here to recapture that vision; to open up our unsatisfactory little souls to the light that pours in through the windows of His holiness. One glance round this evening is quite enough to fill us with that loving penitence for the past and that generous courage for the future which are the best of all dispositions for entering a Retreat. And to-morrow like pilgrims we will go round and make a stand before some of those windows and in their light try to see what we are and what we ought to do. We will take it all very quietly and humbly, try to leave our arguing, critical selves behind. Christianity is not an argument and Christianity is not given us in the form of logic but in the form of beauty and love. We must be receptive, humble and quiet. We must not hunt for imperfections in the windows, for the imperfections may be in our own eyes. If an artist shows you a picture, a musician plays you a Bach prelude, or a man introduces you to his beloved wife, and you fail to perceive their beauty, none of them will argue with you about what you have missed. They would never open your soul that way. And Christianity for the Christian is the perfect picture, the perfect prelude, the perfect bride, only visible to the eyes of humility and love. "A work of art" said Goethe, "is there that we may look at it, not that we may chatter about it." We can look at the Divine work of art in the silence of our Retreat. Perhaps we shall see a beauty we have not seen or guessed before. The treasure hidden in the field was a great treasure; there is something there for everyone. Don't let us spoil our piece by trying to change it into ordinary currency and then grousing about the exchange.

Now each spiritual mystery and truth that is shown to us will have two aspects: one will show us what God in Christ does to and for us, and the other what we, because we are called to incarnate something of the Holy Spirit, must try to do again to and for others. Each represents a gift made to us by God and a demand made on us by God. Religion— Christianity—is like that; a richly living, balanced sequence of gifts and demands. The hallowed thing of Christianity, the media of God's sacramental action are not there only to be looked at and adored like the Ark and the Shewbread of the old Temple, but to be used to give and maintain in us a new kind of life. Water to cleanse us, bread and wine to feed us, oil to consecrate us to His service, nails to pierce us. Christianity, the life of Communion with Christ, means complete and intimate contact between those holy things and our little souls. And we in our turn, cleansed and fed and woven up into the divine society of the Communion of Saints, must give food, light, cleansing, saving, up to the very limit. That is what it means to be a minister of Christ. It is as people called to that, that we have come here, to recapture the beauty and joy of our vocation; by looking at the windows, so convicting in their generosity, so all-demanding in their appeal, and reviewing our lives in their light; letting that light, like healing rays, penetrate our very souls however much it hurts, burning away the hard bits and cleansing the sore bits. It needs courage to expose those bad places and endure the living flame of love that falls on them from the Cross.

Now I think we shall find in our pilgrimage round the Cathedral, as we make a stand before some great aspect of Christ's life and it reveals to us bit by bit the thought of God for man, that there are three things for us to do.

First, looking quietly at the window, bathing in the lovely light that comes through it and which truly gives us God, we shall receive illumination, teaching and healing, a revelation of truth, by absorbing rather than by analysing. The very Light of the Eternal comes to our soul through that vivid Life, showing us the human transfigured by the Divine. That is what St. Ignatius means by contemplating the Mystery of Christ, why he kept saying *Mira! Mira!* Look! Look! Very few people do this properly; they are so anxious to get on to the next stage and be practical. But we shall make our little work of art all the better if we soak our souls in His Beauty first.

That simple contemplation of Christ is a very important part of the life of prayer and our New Testament reading ought to nourish it.

Second (but remember it is second!), we must turn round and apply what we have seen and absorbed to our own inner life which has got to grow up to the fullness of His stature: to put on Christ. He is disclosed both as Saviour and Pattern, especially to those called to the service of Christ. In our daily work and routine, in our religious practice, in our intellectual life with its struggles, tensions, problems and enlightenments; in all these Christ, the Word and Thought of God, is teaching, mending, vivifying us and calling us more and more insistently to love and sacrifice as the only path to union with Him.

In this quiet place, with the windows of His mystery all round us, how do we feel about that? Penitence comes in here for most of us. It is not our own little defects that make us feel most ashamed; it is the vision of Christ. The more enrapt and deliberate our contemplation of the window, the more our little pretensions to Christianity shrink. *There* is God's pattern for humanity and *here* am I. Lord, I am carnal, sold under sin. Nevertheless I come here. I am a bit of your raw material, nothing more. I am to submit and re-submit to your teaching, healing, transfiguring action in order that I may be more useful to your other children. That is what matters. In some way or other each of your states and mysteries concerns my soul and my prayer. I am to think of that. Perhaps in the silence I shall understand it better than before.

Third, but that is not enough. A Christian does not stand alone. As well as the solitude of my soul before God, there is the responsibility of my soul to my fellow-men. As a member of the Mystical Body of Christ, a unit of the Church, I must in some way show these states and characteristics of Christ in my life, some more, some less, according to my special call. I am part of the organism through which Christ continues to live in the world. I too am required to incarnate something of His all-generous and redeeming spirit, share my knowledge of Him, give myself without stint to heal and save other children of God at my own cost. How does my life stand *that* test?

c

There is no getting away from that while we are here! As we turn from one window, we are faced by another always with that convicting and purifying message of holiness and sacrifice and love. And as we come to each, we say with St. Ignatius: What has this to say to me? What light does it cast on my life? What call of God is here for the re-ordering of that life?

I remember once in the Alps finding myself alone in a high pasture surrounded by the strange almost unearthly mountain life. I was filled then with that absolute contentment and solemn happiness which hardly anything else can give to those who have the mountain sense. Above me I could only see the next bit of rough path, but on the other side of the valley I gazed at a great majestic range of snowy peaks and knew they were an earnest of what was above me— waiting for me too if only I would slog on, take a few risks—the hidden reason of the climb with all its hard work. I stood there, getting smaller and smaller and happier and happier as I realized my own place in that great world of beauty and wonder.

Now I think a Retreat should be rather like that: a pause when we can look across the valley and see the great spiritual snowfields in their beauty—Christ and the achievement of the Saints. And although there may seem nothing round us at the moment but shale and rock and scrubby mountain-grass, still we have started and our object, though hidden, is the same.

Wherever we have got to, this experience is always waiting for us, for the Christian life is like one of those mountains with a great many tops. On each apparent summit stands Christ's figure beckoning us on and we think there can be nothing beyond that. But as we struggle up, a further vista opens and beyond it a further height crowned by that same figure, only different, growing and growing in beauty and demand. The figure seems somehow to belong to the mountain and the mountain to the figure; we get less and less able to think of them apart. And at last when we reach the true summit we shall find they are one.

II

INCARNATION AND CHILDHOOD

HERE we come to our first window at the east end of the aisle and the morning light comes through it; the window of the Incarnation. It brings us at once to the mingled homeliness and mystery of the Christian revelation and of our own little lives. It is full of family pictures and ideas—the Birth of Christ, the Shepherds and the Magi, the little boy of Nazareth, the wonderful experience in the Temple, the long quiet years in the carpenter's shop. There seems nothing so very supernatural about the first stage. But stand back and look—*Mira! Mira!*

We are being shown here something profoundly significant about human life—"God speaks in a Son," a Baby Son, and reverses all our pet values. He speaks in our language and shows us His secret beauty on our scale. We have got to begin not by an arrogant other-worldliness, but by a humble recognition that human things can be very holy, very full of God, and that high-minded speculations about His nature need not be holy at all; that all life is engulfed in Him and He can reach out to us anywhere at any level.

As the Christmas Day Gospel takes us back to the Mystery of the Divine Nature—*In the beginning was the Word* . . .—so let us begin by thinking of what St. Catharine called the "Ocean Pacific of the Godhead" enveloping all life. The depth and richness of His being are entirely unknown to us, poor little scraps as we are! And yet the unlimited Life who is Love right through—who loves and is wholly present

36

where He loves, on every plane and at every point—
so loved the world as to desire to give His essential
thought, the deepest secrets of His heart to this small,
fugitive, imperfect creation—to *us*. That seems immense.

And then the heavens open and what is disclosed?
A Baby, God manifest in the flesh. The stable, the
manger, the straw; poverty, cold, darkness—these
form the setting of the Divine Gift. In this Child God
gives His supreme message to the soul—Spirit to
spirit—but in a human way. Outside in the fields the
heavens open and the shepherds look up astonished
to find the music and radiance of Reality all around
them. But inside, our closest contact with that same
Reality is being offered to us in the very simplest,
homeliest way—emerging right into our ordinary
life. A baby—just that. We are not told that the
Blessed Virgin Mary saw the Angels or heard the
Gloria in the air. Her initiation had been quite different, like a quiet voice speaking in our deepest
prayer—"The Lord is with thee!" "Behold the
handmaid of the Lord." Humble self-abandonment
is quite enough to give us God.

Think of the tremendous contrast, transcendent
and homely, brought together here as a clue to the
Incarnation—the hard life of the poor, the absolute
surrender and helplessness of babyhood and the un-
measured outpouring of Divine Life.

Let us take as our first point the story of the Magi.
You know how sometimes on a pitch black night in
the country, you see far off one glimmer of light and
you follow it and it turns out to be just a candle in a
cottage window—but it was enough to assure you of
life ahead, to give you the lead you wanted in the

dark. In the same way, when the Magi turned from their abstruse calculations in search of heaven and followed a star, they did not arrive at a great mathematical result or revelation of the cosmic mind. They found a poor little family party and were brought to their knees—because, like the truly wise, they were really humble-minded—before a baby born under most unfortunate circumstances, a mystery of human life, a little living growing thing. What a paradox! the apparently rich Magi coming to the apparently poor child. There they laid down their intellectual treasures—all pure gold to them—and, better than that, offered the spirit of adoration, the incense which alone consecrates the intellectual life and quest of truth, and that reverent acceptance of pain, mental suffering and sacrifice, that death to self which, like myrrh, hallows the dedicated life in all its forms.

The utmost man can achieve on his own here capitulates before the unspeakable simplicity of the methods of God. After all the shepherds got there long before the Magi and even so, the animals were already in position when the shepherds arrived. He came to His own: the God of nature and of our natural life makes that natural life the material of revelation. The animal world and the natural world have their own rights and their own place within the Thought of God. His light, His smile, kindle the whole universe. He is the Light of the World—all of it. He does not only want or illuminate spiritual things. His hallowing touch is for the ox and the ass, as afterwards for the sparrows and the flowers. There never was a less high-brow religion or one more deeply in touch with natural life than Christianity, although it is infinite in its scope. *Whosoever shall humble himself as this little child, the same shall be greatest in the Kingdom of Heaven.*

It is no use being too clever about life. Only so far as we find God in it do we find any meaning in it. Without Him it is a tissue of fugitive and untrustworthy pleasures, conflicts, ambitions, desires, frustrations, intolerable pain.

Now to accept historical Christianity as God's supreme self-revelation does not mean some elaborate philosophy of the spirit. It means accepting the Gospel story as touching our lives significantly at every point, because it is conveying God. If we are ever to learn all that this record can mean for us, we must never forget that these, beyond all other facts of history, are indwelt, moulded, brought into being by the Living Spirit of God, while plastic to His creative Thought. And if we thus feel God within these events, some so strange and some so homely, inspiring this action and record, then we also accept all these incidents as conveying something of His overruling Will and Thought, having something in them for each of us. Nothing is there by accident. Everything is there because it conveys spiritual truth, gives us the supernatural. It all "speaks to our condition" as Fox would say. The Synoptic Gospels may not always have the accuracy of a photograph but they have a higher reality, they are charged with God. That is the reason why meditation on the Gospels, chewing the evangelical cud, is so nourishing to the soul and so inexhaustible as a basis of prayer. In that sense every word of the Gospel is sacramental; and like some great work of art gives us more and more light and food, revealing greater depths of significance as we grow in the wisdom which is the child of humility and love. The Magi came away from Bethlehem much wiser than they were before.

Now take another point. The Christmas Mystery has two parts: the Nativity and the Epiphany. A deep instinct made the Church separate these two feasts. In the first we commemorate God's humble entrance into human life, the emergence and birth of the Holy, and in the second its manifestation to the world, the revelation of the Supernatural made in that life. And the two phases concern our inner lives very closely too. The first only happens in order that the second may happen, and the second cannot happen without the first. Christ is a Light to lighten the Gentiles as well as the Glory of His people Israel. Think of what the Gentile was when these words were written—an absolute outsider. All cosy religious exclusiveness falls before that thought. The Light of the world is not the sanctuary lamp in your favourite church. It is easy for the devout to join up with the Shepherds and fall into place at the Crib and look out into the surrounding night and say, "Look at those extraordinary intellectuals wandering about after a star, with no religious sense at all! Look at that clumsy camel, what an unspiritual animal it is! *We* know the ox and the ass are the right animals to have! Look what queer gifts and odd types of self-consecration they are bringing; not the sort of people who come to church!" But remember that the Child who began by receiving these very unexpected pilgrims had a woman of the streets for His faithful friend and two thieves for His comrades at the end: and looking at these two extremes let us try to learn a little of the height and breadth and depth of His Love—and then apply it to our own lives.

It was said of Father Wainwright that he cared above all for scamps and drunkards and unbelievers —least for those who came regularly to church—and no man of our time was fuller of the Spirit of Christ. The first point about Epiphany is that *all* are called and welcomed and accepted. Our own loving adoration and deep certitude, if God in His mercy gives us that, is never to break our brotherhood with those who come longer journeys by other paths, led by a different star. The Magi took more trouble than the Shepherds. The intellectual virtues and intellectual longings of men are all blessed in Christ.

And the second point, which every window will bring before us, is that beholding His Glory is only half our job. In our souls too the mysteries must be brought forth; we are not really Christians till that has been done. "The Eternal Birth," says Eckhart, "must take place in *you*." And another mystic says human nature is like a stable inhabited by the ox of passion and the ass of prejudice; animals which take up a lot of room and which I suppose most of us are feeding on the quiet. And it is there between them, pushing them out, that Christ must be born and in their very manger He must be laid—and they will be the first to fall on their knees before Him. Sometimes Christians seem far nearer to those animals than to Christ in His simple poverty, self-abandoned to God.

The birth of Christ in our souls is for a purpose beyond ourselves: it is because His manifestation in the world must be through us. Every Christian is, as it were, part of the dust-laden air which shall radiate the glowing Epiphany of God, catch and reflect His golden Light. *Ye are the light of the world*—but only because you are enkindled, made radiant by the One Light of the World. And being kindled, we have got

to get on with it, be useful. As Christ said in one of
His ironical flashes, "Do not light a candle in order
to stick it under the bed!" Some people make a virtue of religious skulking.

And now let us go on from that, move from the
great central light of the window and see clustering
round it other little lights. The new life grows in
secret. Nothing very startling happens. We see the
Child in the carpenter's workshop. He does not go
outside the frontiers within which He appeared. It
did quite well for Him and will do quite well for us.
There is no need for peculiar conditions in the spiritual
life. Our environment itself, our home and job, are
part of the moulding action of God. Have we fully
realized all that is unfolded in this? How unchris-
tian it is to try to get out of our frame, to separate
our daily life from our prayer? That third-rate little
village in the hills with its limited social contacts
and monotonous manual work reproves us, when we
begin to fuss about opportunities and scope. And
that quality of quietness and ordinariness, that simplicity with which He entered into His great vocation, endured from the beginning to the end. The
Child grows as other children, the Lad works as other
lads. Total abandonment to the vast Divine Purpose
working at its own pace in and through ordinary life
and often, to us, in mysterious ways. I love to think
that much in Christ's own destiny was mysterious to
Him. It was part of His perfect manhood that He
shared our human situation in this too. We seem to
have in the New Testament a record of certain moments when the clouds parted and He saw for a
moment His call and what was at work in Him. "In
that hour He rejoiced . . . I thank Thee, Heavenly

Father . . ." It is the same with us. In a general way we too must go steadily on in pure faith and abandonment to God. When even the Divine mind of Christ looks out from His earthly tabernacle, He seldom gets a very clear view, so why should we presume to demand a clear view? We can't break through the Cloud of Unknowing in which our lives are enfolded. Only the Divine Mind which has conceived each one of our hidden destinies can lead us, but secretly. Like Nicodemus, we come to Him by night.

Now all this should make us realize how deeply hidden and how gradual the soul's growth in the life of prayer must be. It is like the hidden life at Nazareth. We must go on and on doing ordinary things, waiting on God, not trying to stretch ourselves if we are to grow truly and organically in wisdom and stature and in favour with God and man. Growth in God is a far more gradual business than we realize at first. We are so raw and so superficial in our notions; we have no conception of the tremendous changes by which the child of grace becomes the Man of God. All kittens love to behave like cats; but it is no good, and the mouse gets away. We all long to be up and doing long before we are ready to *do*. To contemplate the proportion of Christ's life is a terrible rebuke to spiritual impatience and uppish hurry. There we see how slow according to our time span is the maturing of the thought of God. The higher life's development, the longer is its period of growth. Ephemeral insects become adult in a few moments; the lamb gets up and starts grazing at once; but a baby depends for months on its mother's love. Sanctity, childhood in God, partakes of long divine duration.

We often feel we ought to get on quickly to a new stage like spiritual mayflies. Christ takes thirty years to grow and two and á half to act. The pause, hush, hiddenness which intervene between the Birth and the Ministry are all part of the Divine method. Only the strange dreams Joseph and Mary had, warned a workman and his young wife that they lay in the direct line of God's action, that the growth committed to them mattered supremely to the world. And then, when the growth reached the right stage, there is the revelation of God's call and after it, stress, discipline and choice. "By Thy Baptism, Fasting and Temptation, deliver us." Those things come together as signs of maturity and they are not spectacular things. It is much the same with us in the life of prayer. The Spirit fills us as we grow, develop and make room: He keeps pace with us. He does not suddenly stretch us like a pneumatic tyre with dangerous results. "To contemplate Christ's life," said Augustine, "cures inflation and nourishes humility." How true that is! We see in Him the gradual action of God. He fosters and sanctifies growth, that secret process, especially growth in the hidden interior life which is the unique sign of His own power and of His power in us.

All gardeners know the importance of good root development before you force leaves and flowers. God does not wish you to be one of those lanky plants that grow up too quickly and can't do without a stick. There *are* devout people like that! "Dear Father So-and-so is such a support to me!" But God wants you nice and bushy, rooted and grounded in Him and growing all round, up to the sun, down to the hidden deeps, out to the world. We get notions sometimes that we ought to spring up quickly like seed on stony ground, we ought to show some startling sign of spiritual growth. But perhaps we are only asked to go on quietly, to be a child, a nice stocky seedling, not shooting up in a hurry, but making root, being docile to the great slow rhythm of life. When you don't see any startling marks of your own religious condition or your usefulness to God, think of the Baby in the stable and the little Boy in the streets of Nazareth. The very life was there which was to change the whole history of the human race. There was not much to show for it. But there is entire continuity between the stable and the Easter garden and the thread that unites them is the Will of God. The childlike simple prayer of Nazareth was the right preparation for the awful privilege of the Cross. Just so the light of the Spirit is to unfold gently and steadily within us, till at last our final stature, all God designed for us, is attained. It is an organic process, a continuous Divine action, not a series of jerks. So on the one hand there should be no strain, impatience, self-willed effort in our prayer and self-discipline; and on the other, no settling down. A great flexibility, a gentle acceptance of what comes to us and a still gentler acceptance of the fact that much we see in others is still out of our reach. We must keep our prayer free, frank, youthful—full of confidence and full of initiative too.

The mystics keep telling us that the goal of that prayer and the goal of that hidden life which should itself become more and more of a prayer, is "union with God." We use that phrase often, much too often to preserve the wholesome sense of its awe-fulness. For what does union with God mean? It is not a nice feeling we get in devout moments. That may or may not be a by-product of union—probably not.

It can never be its substance. Union with God means every bit of our human nature transfigured in Christ, woven up into His creative life and activity, absorbed into His redeeming purpose, heart, soul, mind and strength. Each time it happens it means that one of God's creatures has achieved its destiny.

And if men and women want to know what this means in terms of human nature, what it costs and what it becomes, there is only one way—contemplation of the life of Christ. Then we see that we grow in wisdom and stature not just for our own sakes— just to become spiritual—but that His teaching, healing, life-giving power may possess us and work through us; that we may lose our own lives and find His life, be conformed to the Pattern shown in Him, conformed to the Cross. Those are the rich and costly demands and experiences that lie before us as we stand at the first window and look at the Child setting up a standard for both simple and learned, teaching the secrets of life; and what they ask from us on our side and from our prayer is a very great simplicity, self-oblivion, dependence and suppleness, a willingness and readiness to respond to life where it finds us and to wait, to grow and change, not according to our preconceived notions and ideas of pace, but according to the overruling Will and Pace of God.

III

Now let us look up at Christ, the Word of God, the living Thought of God, beginning His career of loving service, going about His Father's business which is the only real business of man and not very spectacular. Ordinary life, love, devotedness will do quite well for the revealing action of God. St. Mark says, "They went into Capernaum and straightway on the Sabbath Day He entered into the synagogue and taught. And they were astonished at His doctrine for He taught them as one having authority and not as the scribes."

So if Christ's first call must ever be to a humble child-like response in which there is something of the simplicity of Bethlehem and Nazareth and if the first thing He asks of all of us is a new birth into a new order, a life in which all centres on God—His next demand is to those who ignore their own spiritual profit and offer themselves as channels for the message of God to men. In one way or another, in real disciples, the two things go together. Real disciples are always apostles too: only the humble and childlike towards God, those who are receptive and have been long trained in lowliness, can be trusted to teach or show others the truth about God. For all teaching that is worth anything is an effect of charity, devoted to God and, for His sake, to the children of God. In one way or another we are all pupil-teachers, working for love. We have freely received and because of that, freely give again. Never

47

hoard the spiritual treasure! Give all the time! That
principle runs through Christ's life. The humble,
childlike, self-abandoning prayer on the mountain
is the necessary source of all that is given with
authority in the synagogue and on the shore. And it
is our humble childlike reception of Him which
alone gives us the power to teach. For some, of
course, the whole of Christ's life is one great dramatic
lesson. He taught by His visible presence and
teaches by His invisible presence still. He teaches by
His own silent transcendence of our universal failure,
our self-occupation, pessimism, jealousy, conceit,
ambition; shows us these things for what they are.
He teaches by and in His Church, His Sacraments,
His Saints: all alive because united with His Spirit—
Lo! I am with you always! He shows us what a life
is like that has really been reborn in the Divine order,
entirely subordinate to the interests of God. We see
in Him its nature and quality and inevitable sequence,
how it handles life, what it effects and how.

All this is just what we want to know if we are to
rise above our confusion and be effective agents of His
work. It is not an easy syllabus. Temptation at the
beginning—many never get further than that—and
Gethsemane very near the end. And in thus teaching
us He uses the whole web of life, as in the synagogue.
He still unrolls the great scroll of history and lights
that up; and sometimes the small secret scroll of our
own inner history, generally kept rolled up tight because we don't very much care to look at it. He
comes and unrolls it in all its shabbiness with all its
odious record of wrong things, cheap things, persis-
tent self-love and self-interest, chances of generosity
missed, love we failed to value, sacrifices we did not
make. He opens that roll and reads from it and we

realize for the first time what a hash we have made of our chance of Christlikeness and what that really means over against God. That is one of the most purifying, abasing and bracing experience which can happen to a soul. Christ teaches contrition to His poor little pupil helpers and slaves. Our past sins and mistakes, seen thus, teach us the humbling lesson of our own great frailty and so throw us back on God. If we take them the right way they can at least cure our cocksureness and that is a great gain. If we look back on the days when we were bright young creatures and thought we understood life, perhaps it will cure us of the suspicion that we really do understand it now.

So He can use the lessons of the past, the scroll which records all our jumbled memories, to teach us self-knowledge. And self-knowledge compelled by Christ is the only path to a real life-giving penitence, for it is only when He unrolls that scroll with His own hands—"His holy and venerable hands" as the ancient prayer of consecration says—that we learn what sin is, by contrast with His compassionate, self-giving holiness; the holiness of One in perfect accord with God, who teaches with the absolute and unselfconscious authority, the disconcerting realism of the channel of God—not the priggish exactitude of the moralist and critic of society. And He teaches us just where we are, in our own synagogue, our own boat, our own town, or just where we catch up with Him by the side of the lake or in the hills. He uses all the stuff of our everyday life, the forms of everyday religion, as His school material: that everyday life familiar to all, yet having a sacred significance no one can ever exhaust. And so He always moves easily and safely between the

D

two extremes which threaten the teacher—the temptation to aim at easy shallow popularity on the one hand or at a difficult exclusive superiority on the other.

Each gets from Him what they need because He always thinks of them, not of His own doctrine and Person or the novelty and importance of His message. Those who are called to be His pupil-teachers in the world to-day must think a little about this. Just look at that beautiful absence of rigorism, that gentle, flexible, life-giving method which is yet never sentimental, vague or soft. Consider what humbleness, what reverence for our human nature it involves; in one line it is and has the Truth of God. Look at the willingness to give milk to babes because they are babes; not to risk spiritual indigestion by trying to make them tackle a square meal of pure truth. Christ never seems at first sight to be giving pure truth; yet in the end He is the only teacher who manages to give it in a way that feeds souls of every level and type. Wherever He comes, He brings the life-giving mystery of God: but giving the mystery in and with the homeliness, weaving together both worlds.

What a lesson for us! And especially for those who have a secret arrogant craving for what they call "purely spiritual things." There is nothing abstract or high-brow about Him. To all He gives parables capable of simple interpretation and to some revelations within them of the Mysteries of the Kingdom of Heaven. There is no overfeeding or straining of souls and, above all, no hurry to enlighten at all costs everyone He can reach. What a great supernatural art that is—that quiet, humble patience; whether of those who teach or of those being taught. Whichever class we think we are in, we are all studying under the quiet eye of God; and we have got to learn the artist's pace, never to hurry or scramble or lose our breath, yet never to wait too long; to put on a good primary coat and *let it dry* in spite of our eagerness to get on with the picture before the inspiration fades; the only result of which is a sticky mess.

Christ seems so often content to prepare souls by one great revealing truth and then just leave grace to act, to fertilize, to bring forth, to give light with that easy generosity and not ask about results. To leave it to God, to make no effort to harvest one's own corn and say, "See what a lot of sheaves *I* have brought in!"—that asks for a self-oblivion which is very near the Cross.

Look at the Parable of the Sower, and remember it is the Sower Himself who speaks. Anyone who cares for a garden, or is sensitive to the life of the fields, knows how near in sowing and planting we feel to the Mystery of God, how we seem to enter His rhythm, share a bit of His creative joy in a way appropriate to our humble state.

And now see what it seems in the eyes of the perfect Sower, the one Divine Teacher. He puts first all the wasted effort—and acknowledges it *is* wasted— then all the disappointing results, all the things the teacher has against him, the poor and shallow soil, the competing interests, the hostile influences choking the development of the seed. All these have to be reckoned with. The Sower goes forth without bitterness or reluctance knowing all that and slogs steadily on. The handful of successes comes last—but makes it all worth while.

We often have to carry on under the same conditions: misunderstanding, shallow appreciation, rejection of all that is not popular or easy, waste of the seed we know to be good—"From that time many went back and followed Him no more." Self-esteem sowing its own seed soon crumples under the test. If we are asked in our tiny way—and every Christian is—to help with the sowing, we had better get the conditions well into our minds, face reality.

Now take another point. The teaching action of God penetrates, of course, all life and is felt by us in all sorts of ways. We are often taught, like children, through our toys. There is a lot of kindergarten work to be done in the spiritual world. Just as the toy-engine and toy-animal wake interest and train children in method and care, so we can develop and train a zest, a skill and love meant for great purposes by a careful and devoted use of them for small purposes. So too all the obstacles and resistances of life and of our own temperaments are part of the educational material of Christ. They teach us an ever-greater dependence on Him and an ever greater sympathy with our brothers and sisters who are being trained and tested in the same way. We are inclined to say, "If I had a different psychological outfit, if I had not inherited Grandpapa's unfortunate temper or had not got Uncle John's dreadfully prosaic mind —if my mind did not always wander when saying my prayers—if my daily routine were not so exacting, and if I could always get a quiet time in the morning, be clear of the telephone and callers and other things I ought to be doing—in fact if I could shed my whole physical and mental apparatus and get another lot better adjusted to a minister of Christ—or else if I could become purely spiritual, *then* I might progress in the knowledge and love of God and power for His service."

That is one of the silliest mistakes we can possibly make. All this apparatus is just school furniture which contributes to educate us in real knowledge and love of God, contempt for self, utter dependence on Him—things we can only learn through life. "Books," said St. Augustine after his conversion, "could not teach me charity." We still keep on thinking they can. We do not realize nearly enough the utter distinctness of God and the things of God. Psychology of religion cannot teach us prayer, and ethics cannot teach us love. Only Christ can do that and He teaches by the direct method, in and among the circumstances of life. He does not mind about our being comfortable. He wants us to be strong, able to tackle life and be Christians, be apostles in life, so we must be trained by the ups and downs, the rough and tumble of life. Team games are compulsory in the school of Divine Love; there must be no getting into a corner with a nice spiritual book.

Look at it another way. When we consider the immense demands made on us, on our courage, initiative, patience, compassion, by the natural life we live here (if we take it as we should), what will be the demands, tensions, mighty opportunities of love and service offered to the mature soul by the life of the Eternal World? We are being educated by Christ the Teacher for that world as well as this. You don't think Heaven will be soft chairs and Vi-springs, do you? Christ the teacher trains us for Heaven, the Kingdom of God, and links the Kingdom of God with the most homely and practical tests and duties and experiences; He never leaves them out.

Are we taking our lives like that, paying attention to the lessons, both those that interest and delight us and those we find dull and hard?

Our firm and gentle Teacher never ceases His efforts to show us the Mystery of the Kingdom of God in the life of field and house, city and mountain, through shepherds and merchants, children and craftsmen. It is left to us to respond, to be alert, to look and listen and do our home work with a full sense of responsibility; and only in so far as we do it shall we be satisfactory teachers in our turn. We must do it with faith and hope because, like children learning Latin grammar, it is often very difficult for us to see at that stage what possible good it can be or realize the splendour of the world it is going to open up, the deep meaning it will give to life.

Here we are all held tight in the complex sort of existence we have built up—electrically lit and mechanically warmed and fuller and fuller of intricate needs and aids—and yet for all that its mysterious realities are no more understood: only we are mostly too busy rushing about to stop and realize these mysterious realities.

In a Retreat we do stop. Then we see how little we know that really matters, how spiritually uneducated we are, that all our modest knowledge leaves the deeps of existence unexplored. The soul is still very like the sparrow that flew through the lighted hall from dark to dark. We are inclined to ignore all that, leave it out; if we then fly like an incautious airman, we may get into a spin if we leave the solid earth too far behind. We like to think of the "warm humanity" of the Gospel as we call it and represent this as the essence of the teaching of Christ. We must not do that. It is not Christian to leave the Mystery out. Christ does not leave it out. His teaching has a deep recurring note of awe, a solemn sense of God and the profound mystery of God. His abrupt

entry into human life, coming to us and judging us
in every crisis—grief, shock, sacrifice—flashing up on
life's horizon like lightning just when we have settled
down on the natural level and casting over the land-
scape a light we had never dreamed of before—the
light of His judgments, choices, separations, demands.
The whole teaching of Christ hinges on God as the
supreme factor in every situation from the tiniest to
the most universal. *Watch for ye know not the hour.*
God said, *This night thy soul shall be required of thee.
. . . The last shall be first and the first last. . . . The
chaff shall be burnt. . . .* The clue to life He offers is
not a bit of soft ribbon but a hard rope that will bear
our weight but will also chafe our hands!

The apocalyptic passages in the Gospel worry
people sometimes. What do they come to? Surely
a sense of the deep mystery and awful significance of
our existence conveyed in the picturesque language
of the East. The immense span of His understanding
goes from the lilies of the field to the terrible and
mysterious movements of history when "men's hearts
fail them from fear and for looking after the things
which are coming on the earth." He takes all that in,
the darkness and anxiety of our situation, whether
corporate or personal, and within and beyond all He
finds God, the One Reality, the One Life. Perhaps
there we have got to the root of the matter. Christ
teaching in His life and death, in His Scriptures and
His Church and Saints, and secretly with each soul
in prayer—all different aspects of one action, parts
of His economy and so charged with His life—teaching but one thing, GOD, and our total self-giving to
God—God who is greater than our heart. Once we
have truly learned that lesson all else falls into place.

And the lesson cannot be given in a series of propositions. Here words are merely carriers of the secret supernatural communication, the light and call of God. This is why spiritual books bear such different meanings for different types and qualities of soul, why each time we read them they give us something fresh, as we can bear it. Such books and teachers are reservoirs of the Spirit; what they give us is nothing to what they still hold in reserve. Just as the children who "do" Shakespeare in the lower forms, get what they can assimilate without even guessing all that is left over, waiting for the growth of their minds. The New Testament, the Psalms, all the great literature of the Spirit is like that. As St. Gregory said: "Elephants can swim in it and lambs can paddle." For through it God's communication, the living Ocean of His Love, is given to all His children whatever their size and capacity.

Christ's parables are like that, inexhaustible to us, charged with supernatural suggestion, yet ever on their surface giving a homely wisdom all can understand. The Lord's Prayer is the classical example of this, containing in itself the whole substance of His teaching. Every baby can give some meaning to it; no saint has exhausted its meaning. As the life of prayer deepens, so those phrases get more and more charged with significance, more and more carry us towards God, so it gets more and more difficult to get to the end of it in a reasonable time. In it Christ shows us man's blessedness and the path that leads to it; immense and glad dependence and confidence as towards God, utter surrender to the Will of God.

This is that Life Eternal which, by example and precept, Christ the Teacher brings to every soul.

IV

CHRIST THE HEALER

WHEN our Lord sent forth the seventy to proclaim the Kingdom of God, they were to do it by teaching, by healing the sick and by rescuing from the clutch of evil. Those three streams of active love are still poured out through the Church on us and those three obligations still lie on all His chosen agents. This morning we thought of Christ the Teacher and what He gives us and asks from us. Now we go on to Christ the Healer, whose ministers we are, and the healing, cherishing, merciful action of God, His loving-kindness always reaching out, as it were, through His creatures to His creatures. That healing, restoring action is one of the loveliest strands in Christianity; it runs right through it and is the essence of what we mean by salvation—body, mind and spirit. That generous, spendthrift giving of health, power, new life which runs through the Gospels, reveals to us the untiring loving-kindness, the deep compassion for all imperfection, suffering and failure, which dwells in the heart of Reality and must colour our lives if we are indeed to be Children of God and of the Light.

If the first effect of the Love of Christ in us is to teach us life's meaning and how to live it, if He first appears to us as the Way, the Truth and the Life, He now appears as the Physician of souls too maimed and sick without Him to take up that life, to tread that way. So the Incarnate Thought of God teaches us how to live: trains, guides, enlightens us. The fostering mercy tempers that stern and lovely radiance, restores and mends us, makes us able to live, opens the eyes of the blind and the ears of the deaf, restores impotent and crippled souls, brings us back to the right line, to health.

Some people are rather troubled about the amount of space the healing of the sick takes in the Gospels. Teaching and healing between them take the whole centre of the record, practically cover the ministry. Perhaps we feel that is not quite spiritual enough for the supernatural revelation of God to man. This is because we are apt to think of healing as getting rid of people's normal pain, disease, disability, distress. But healing is really restoring to the true normality, restoring to full manhood, mending the breaches in our perfect humanity, and making us again what God intends us to be. It shows us His life-giving Spirit; the Lord and Giver of Life ever at work producing and restoring fullness of life. For all disease of soul or body is a subtraction from human nature, a way of being sub-standard. There are no colds in Paradise. So, healing of any sort is a kind of creative or rather regenerating work, a direct expression and furtherance of God's Will. It means bringing life back to what it ought to be, mending that which has broken down, healing our deep mental and spiritual wounds by the action of His charity, giving new strength to the weak, new purity to the tainted.

And this is not only part of God's character; it is also a definite characteristic of every human soul's vocation as declared in Christ. In one form or another it has got to be present in our lives. His healing loving-kindness has got to flow through us if we are really self-given to Him. You know the great

Confraternity of the Misericordia in Italy to which men of all classes belong, in which all are equal and every member liable to be called out in the service of the sick and dying. We are all by our baptism members of the Misericordia of Christ, all "menders" of His creatures; all givers of health and light whether to body, mind or spirit. All those in whom His passion for bringing things back to normal is at work are part of the great healing action of His Mystical Body.

So, too, right through the created order. It is one of the forms taken by the self-outpouring of the Perfection of God to His imperfect creation. Every healing action is always God's, but He often takes something of ours or something we think is ours to do it with—His is the power, skill and tenderness; ours to yield up our best handkerchief for His bandages, our leisure to carry out His treatment. We must silence our disgust at the patient He may ask us to help with and the sort of thing He sometimes wants done. St. Francis who healed the worst misery of the leper by conquering his own revulsion for that dreadful countenance and giving him the kiss of brotherhood; St. Vincent de Paul telling his ladies of Charity to serve the sick poor in their filthy Paris garrets with the reverence and courtesy due to the representative of Christ—these are in the right line; healing love flowed through them without impediment.

St. Jerome, laying aside his writing and giving his whole attention to taking the disabling thorn from the lion's paw, really *is* a Saint, a tool of God: far more so than when writing controversial letters to those who did not agree with him about theology. A good veterinary surgeon is one of the instruments of Divine Love. That divine life and light which is born in every soul surrendered to God has healing in its wings.

Let us take, as the starting-point of our meditation, Christ's healing of the sick of the palsy (St. Mark ii, 1–12). Look at the poor, shaky nerve-ridden creature, utterly jangled, all to bits, at odds with physical and mental life, brought into the atmosphere of the Holy in a last desperate attempt to find a cure. Those who carried him in—and in their passion of sympathy broke the roof in order to get through—had their share in the cure. They made the contact for that helpless nerveless thing by their initiative and determination. Those qualities, too, enter into the healing order of God. I suppose we may think of the man sick of the palsy as an advanced neurotic, ravaged and destroyed by his unhappy phobias, fears and obsessions. Christ goes straight to the spiritual root of the situation. He does not reprove the poor wretch—"Leave off behaving like this! Pull yourself together!"—but pours out the steady radiance of His health-giving charity, bracing and pacifying, releasing from the clutch of the past. "It is all right! Fear not! Your sins are done away! The love of God, so much stronger than your fears, restores you to your old place, your normality. You are reinstated. So, rise and resume the full life of a human being! Pick up the mat on which you have been carried in! That's all over. Look forward and not backward! *Walk!*"

That is our model for dealing with the results of weakness and sin. The patient is really a moral invalid, the type of all nerve-ridden impotent souls defeated by circumstances and worn by inner conflicts, restored to his full stature by the healing power of God and his own act of faith in that healing power. In every healing act of Christ, the patient's own will must be called out to complete the cure. "Immediately he rose up·before them," says St. Luke, "and took up that whereon he lay and departed to his own house, glorifying God." He had recognized and accepted the gift of healing love and was not under the weather any more. His psychological renovation was complete. His full manhood, responding to God and His human world, was restored and brought into play. That alone is health. Even the influenza patient is not cured while he still crawls about saying, "You see I have had a touch of 'flu!" but only when he forgets all about it and gets on with his normal life. In the same way when the healing touch of Christ is laid on our souls, His real successes are not those grateful patients who never forget how ill they have been and are terribly afraid of another temperature: they are the ones whose faith and gratitude make them forget themselves and their poor little sins, who stand up and glorify God and go forward in the new energy of His power and love, dropping themselves and their unfortunate past. Some of the greatest of the Saints are among Christ's moral cures—from Mary Magdalene to Charles de Foucauld—but they always look forward, not backward, with a wonderful combination of fresh vigorous initiative and absolute and grateful trust. People who "enjoy bad health" whether spiritual or physical will never respond to His healing power with the fullness and faith He asks.

Now as we look at each of Christ's Mysteries—and each one is so wonderful that for the time being we think its revelation is complete—we feel it seems to demand of us two movements, a movement of prayer and a movement of service. We all need in one way

or another that which is here poured out of the life
and love of God, and that same light and love require
of us, in our turn, a total self-giving to its purposes.
These two movements of dependence on Christ and
co-operation with Him make together a Christian's
life. We can only give what we have received, we
only receive in order to give. "Charity seeketh not
her own"—not even her own spiritual well-being.
St. Augustine's prayer sums it up—"Give what you
demand of me and then ask what you will!" That
is: Deliver me, God of my health! And then accept
me as your servant. Take all I have and use it in
your great redeeming and healing work. "As poor
yet making many rich"—Christianity alone gives us
that paradoxical formula of a life hidden in God.

So now look at this picture and at that Figure
which dominates it and all the helpless victims of
the world's disharmony and the soul's disharmonies
who lie at His feet. And think first of His healing,
restoring action and presence in our own lives; our
desperate need of it in small things and in great;
the practical impossibility of getting through without it and how this fact keeps us humble before God.

Let us look into our minds and souls. Could we
claim a clean bill of health? Is our whole psychical
and spiritual machinery running right, quite adjusted
and adequate to circumstances? No old wounds to
self-esteem that give us twinges? No auto-intoxica-
tion of jealousy, resentment, depression quietly going
on? No acidity? No displacements, adhesions, no
chronic ailments? Are we fit, as His agents should be,
for all weathers, all jobs? "Try me, O God, and seek
the ground of my heart," says the Psalmist. Prove
me, examine my reactions. "Look well if there be

any way of wickedness in me and lead me in the way everlasting." That kind of internal examination may be very painful, shameful, searching; but only those willing to submit to it can hope for the full healing of Christ. His diagnosis comes before His treatment.

All sin is disease. It takes many forms. Some of us seem liable to intermittent fevers; some to self-poisoning by pride and self-love, which are always thwarting our perfect adjustment to life. We can't produce the right anti-toxin ourselves. He must enter our lives with His spirit of humility and renunciation and cleanse us of infection; must blend His spirit with our spirit to give us of His health. So, too, He heals our jangled and distracted minds, our turbulent desires and conflicts, by the infusion of His peace: all the scratches life has made on our souls, that general sensation of soreness and stiffness and uneasiness which reduces our natural power of adjustment to life: the terrible spiritual insomnia in which we toss and find no rest, those torturing devils so easy for the overdriven modern to believe in—somehow, we don't know how, He gives us release. They are all cast out by the sanity of holiness. "Christ," says à Kempis, "establishes us in God by making us think on such things as cause inward peace of soul." Not, of course, unless we want it, want it so much that we cease our struggles and abandon ourselves to His power. The self-abandoned prayer which ceases its own struggles and its own patent medicines and places itself with entire confidence in His hand, alone opens up paths for His healing energy. "Lord, if Thou wilt Thou canst. Say the word only. I know you can say it. Have mercy! Cast forth my particular private devil. I can't."

So, too, if we hand ourselves over with confidence

and without reserve He will exercise on us His pre-
ventive medicine, simplify our lives, teach us what to
do and what to leave out, persuade us to a plainer,
more regular, more wholesome spiritual diet. Many
souls go on and on suffering in a dull way from
chronic indigestion and wonder why they never feel
quite right. "Just a ten minutes' reading of the New
Testament and perhaps a bit of St. Teresa and a
chapter of Higher Criticism (intellectually so important) and that Office I am bound by the Guild Rules
to say. And my self-examination of course and perhaps a bit of Mr. So-and-so's helpful little book. And
I must not forget the social side of Christianity! And
then five minutes' silence—but I haven't time for
more."

And yet, this hastily absorbed selection of odds
and ends is only required to serve one simple
purpose—to feed our God-ward lives—and the only
thing that matters is that it shall contain the essential foodstuffs that do that. There is a biochemistry
of the soul and it is surely part of our religious duty
to arrange our religious meals in accordance with its
laws and with some care; to take what really
nourishes us and take it under conditions which
help us to relish and digest our food. A good spiritual
writer is like a good cook who dishes up food in a
suitable way—but the food itself is Divine. As a
certain wise Prioress said, "Most books on religion
have thousands of words—we need only one word,
GOD—and that surrounded not by many words but
by silence." Christ, the soul's healer, gives us or
will give us that word which quiets our fever, feeds,
steadies and deepens our life, builds up our resistance
to the toxins which get into our blood-stream and sap
our powers.

And so we turn to ourselves and ask, how does the mysterious light from this window illumine and reprove our attitude, our lives, our work, our prayer? For as Members of Christ, Ministers of Christ, we are committed to take our part in His healing action in the world.

And first, do we think our touch on life—not Life with a capital L which is a mere abstract but the actual lives which touch our own, the lives of our own people, our immediate circle—do we think our lives have in them that outflowing, healing compassion? Do those who come into contact with us go away more or less jangled than before? More vigorous or less? More sure of God or less? Are we conveying Christ or the opposite? A stream of vague depression seems to spread from some people like fog from a marsh—that is terrible in a Christian. What *ought* to spread from us is a bit of the Divine healing love, giving itself, its power and interest without stint to those who need it, whether on the physical, mental or spiritual plane.

Now it means an immense self-emptying if we are to take up our part in this spiritual healing ministry of the Body of Christ. Whether given on a great scale to heal the world's disease and sin or on a small scale to the devoted care of an individual soul, it is always a sacrificial job: all-demanding, costly, mortifying self-interest and self-love even in their most subtle and spiritual forms. It has been said that a ceaseless death to self is asked of all light-bearing souls, and this is a hundred times more true of healing souls. We must ignore our pains and preferences, our own longing for sympathy and peace, our times of weakness, anguish, desolation, fatigue; we must go

E

on giving, up to the limit and beyond. Christ Himself groaned in spirit at the effort demanded of Him. He knew what virtue had gone out; He gave a costly, not an easy restoration to the fallen and weak. He bore our burdens and carried our sorrows.

How do we feel about that? To go where healing love is needed, and give it in a way in which it can be received, often means acting in the teeth of our own interests and preferences, even religious interests and preferences. Christ risked His reputation for holiness by healing on the Sabbath; He touched the unclean, dined with the wrong people; He accepted the love and companionship of a sinner (that most wonderful of all remedies for the wounds of sin). He loved with God's love and so went straight to the point: What can I do to restore my fellow-creature and how?

When we replace disinterested healing love by self-interested devotion, when we neglect the needs of the sinful and helpless because they conflict with our religious or moral ideas, when we elude the intimate companionship of the Magdalene and the leper, the nerve-ridden clutch of the possessed and all the variety of psychological wrecks which strew the modern scene in their restless loneliness—then we neglect the interest of God in the interest of our own spiritual comfort. Religious individualists and rigorists should think well of this. It is true that God is the unique source of all the healing energies in life. But as He reached out through Christ, so He still reaches out through men and women and often asks us to pay for part of His treatments. If a T.B. patient requires an open window our contribution may be putting up with the draught. If those from whom He cast out devils depended for continuous health on being with Christ, the disciples of Christ had to accept their companionship. One often wonders what those pious fishermen thought about it when the Magdalene joined the group. Healing love must drop all personal choices and preferences, all fastidiousness, all desire to get something out of our union with Christ; and be willing to work for nothing, be a faithful servant, not a pet. We may have to see all the resources of Divine Love poured out on a damaged and undeserving Prodigal, the fatted calf, the music and dancing—while *we* are left in the unemotional and hard-working position of the elder son. Only perfect self-oblivion is going to handle that situation well. "Son, thou art ever with me and all that I have is thine. But only if you use it as I use it; come in with me as a partner, pour it out without stint in spendthrift generosity on those who *need* restoration and healing, not those who *deserve* it."

If our call to share the life of Christ the Teacher lays the Cross upon the intellect, our call to share the life of Christ the Healer lays the Cross upon the heart.

V

CHRIST THE RESCUER

"THEN He arose, and rebuked the wind and the raging of the water: and they ceased, and there was a calm" (St. Luke viii, 24). Or as St. Mark says (vi, 47–51), perhaps giving another memory of that same incident:

> And when even was come, the ship was in the midst of the sea, and He alone on the land. And he saw them toiling in rowing, for the wind was contrary to them: and about the fourth watch of the night He cometh unto them, walking upon the sea, and would have passed by them. But when they saw Him walking upon the sea, they supposed it had been a spirit, and cried out: for they all saw him, and were troubled. And immediately He talked with them, and saith unto them, Be of good cheer: it is I; be not afraid. And He went up unto them into the ship; and the wind ceased: and they were sore amazed in themselves. . . .

That is the window we are looking at this morning. It marks, I think, a transition to a fresh level, fresh depths of Divine revelation in Christ, a fresh disclosure of man's need of God and a fresh demand on the ministers of God.

As we make our pilgrimage round the Cathedral, each fresh stand seems at first as if it completed the story. And for some souls it does, at least for a time. Christ, the revelation and thought of God indwelling our world, living our life, teaches us His wisdom about life and heals the wounds of life. At first we think that is what the world needs and that is enough. But after a bit, as we get to know our weakness and as life batters and maims us, we know we all badly need mending before we can fully profit by the lessons of the teacher. If we stop there, at the perfect Teacher and Healer, solving the problems and healing the diseases of our strange and difficult existence and calling for our co-operation even in His work—that sort of humanitarian Christianity which is so popular to-day and which is already the loveliest thing within our world—if we don't look beyond it, it seems complete. But it is less than half the total illumination given us by God in Christ; we are here only just reaching the fringe of His mystery and greatness and full demand. God enters human life not only to help, teach and complete it, but to overrule, transform, rescue and control circumstance—a saving energy intervening with an entire and noble freedom, constrained only by love. *Kyrie Eleison! Christe Eleison!* Lord have mercy! Christ have mercy! We appeal to One who has power to save and to change. "The Son of Man is Lord even of the Sabbath Day," says Christ to the Jewish rigorists, surely with an ironic smile. "Who is this" say the disciples caught in the tempest, "that even the winds and waves obey Him?"

The teaching of men how to live, the healing and reviving touch on their weakness and disease, might have come from a non-Christian revelation of reality. But more than that flows out to us from the eternal life of Christ within His Church. We cannot live long within the aura of that life without experiencing something that comes in, breaking in from beyond the natural order, to save, change, direct and feed us —an intervening power—the merciful stooping down of Perfection to enter into His little creature's affairs, the energetic rescuing action of the Eternal Christ.

Look at this picture. You see the stormy lake and the little boat with its low freeboard and shallow draught, just as used on the Lake of Galilee now, and the frightened faces of the fishermen. And standing above them the solitary and tranquil figure of Christ ruling the storm; more than that, for through and in that storm He is revealed to them as never before. We never realize that power in full until we too are caught and threatened by the violence and hostility of events or the frightful storms of our own unstable natures. It is then that His mysterious action is felt within the circumstances of our lives. . . . "And He went up unto them into the ship; and the wind ceased: and they were sore amazed.. . . ."

Sometimes we are as it were in the middle of the lake and the storm breaks, usually from a quarter we don't expect, and we are doubtful whether the little boat is going to stand it. We feel helpless, making no progress and are inclined to say: "I have gone to bits; I have no help, no support. *This* cannot be a spiritual life." We begin to lose our grip. The boat is very cranky and unstable, the waves very threatening and steep, the sky darkening, we are in utter wretchedness and discouragement.

It was like that when He "went up unto them into the ship and the wind ceased". Then the situation was transformed by His presence. One way or another, life brings every awakening Christian soul this experience. When we recognize and reflect on it— for it may come in a way that seems very simple—it fills us with awe and grateful love. God in Christ intervenes between us and the storm that threatens to overwhelm us. His power is brought into action just where our action fails; He comes to the rescue of those caught in the toils of circumstance.

. This is a secret that has always been known to men and women of prayer, something we can trust and that acts in proportion to our trust. Sometimes it is on our soul that He lays His tranquillizing touch and stills the storm; sometimes on the hurly-burly of our emotional life, sometimes on events that we think must destroy us or the people and causes we love and who are mysteriously modified by the Spirit that indwells and overrules them. We do feel sometimes as if we are left to ourselves to struggle with it all. He is away praying on the mountain, or He is asleep in the boat; the waves seem to be getting decidedly higher, the night is very dark and we don't feel sure about our gear—we begin to lose our nerve for life and no one seems to mind. Certainly life is not made soft for Christians; but it *is*, in the last resort, safe. The universe is safe for souls. The disciples were thoroughly frightened, exhausted, soaked to the skin, but *not* destroyed. At the critical moment He went up into the ship and restored safety, sanity, peace. So, too, when the four thousand were hungry and without resources and the disciples got very worried about it. But they *were* all fed and fed in an entirely unexpected way. So Christ stands over against history and in its darkest and most dangerous moments we receive a new revelation of His power.

We can never forecast the path God's energy of rescue will take. It is never any use saying to Him, "I am getting desperate! Please answer my prayer by the next post and please send an open cheque." He *will* answer but not necessarily like that; more probably He will transform and use the unlikely-looking material already in hand—the loaves and the tiny fishes—looking up to Heaven and blessing it and making it do after all. A priest was once asked if many miracles happened at Lourdes. He said, "Yes, many; but the greatest are not miracles of healing but the spiritual miracles, the transformation of those who pray desperately for cure of this or that and come back, not physically cured, but filled with peace and joy, surrendered to the Will of God, conformed to the Cross."

He entered the ship and the wind ceased, and there was a calm.

So this meditation sheds a tranquil radiance on all our lives; teaches us in the stress and difficulty of these lives, in conflict with circumstance, in all the tight places to which we are brought in our work, to look for and trust the rescuing and supporting action of God—so seldom exerted in the way we think it must be exerted, yet always present, always intervening in the real interests of the souls He loves. If Christianity sometimes seems hard, it is the hardness of a great enterprise in which we get great support. More and more as we go on with the Christian life we learn the strange power of the Spirit over circumstance; seldom sensationally declared but always present and active—God in His richness and freedom coming as a factor into every situation, overruling the ceaseless stream of events which make up our earthly existence and, through those events, moulding our souls. The radiation of His love penetrates, modifies, quickens our lives.

This general action of the Power of God in life is what we rather vaguely call Providence. Its pressure and action is continuous in and through the texture of that life but usually it is unseen. It conditions our whole career from birth to death just as the invisible lines of force within a magnetic field condition all the tiny iron filings scattered on it. But now and then it does emerge on the surface and startles us by its witness to a subtle and ceaseless power and love working within the web of events. I am sure we ought to think of this far more than we do. When instances of its action are collected as in *The Holy and the Living God*,[1] we are astonished at their impressiveness. This sort of evidence of the direct action of God lies very thick on the pages of the New Testament, sometimes intervening in great and crucial events, sometimes in very homely things like the shortage of wine at the wedding made good and the situation saved, sometimes in desperate crises like the storm quelled just in time, the chosen servants of God brought safely through danger, the prison doors opened. "The power of God unto salvation," says St. Paul (not the power of God unto comfort) is the essence of the Gospel, a personal energy, a never-ceasing Presence that intervenes and overrules events.

I don't know why we think this strange. It is just our dull unimaginative stuffiness. Even on our tiny human scale, we feel that the perfect master of a great industry is one who organizes the whole in the interest of good and profitable work and of the well-being of the workers, who gives his subordinates a relative freedom and lets the factory run on ordained lines without too much interference in details. Yet he is always accessible to the personal troubles and desires of his workers, overrides rules where necessary and is interested in every detail down to the factory

[1] *The Holy and the Living God*, by M. D. R. Willink. George Allen & Unwin, 1931.

cat. Even one human creature can do that without surprising us. But when Christ says the Absolute Majesty and Holiness of God can both rule heaven and care for the sparrow and will intervene to help and save, we think that is poetry and paradox, and stories about it are superstitions. We are too stupid and too narrow in our notions to conceive the energy of the Unmeasurable Holy, entering our world, changing and modifying circumstance.

Yet we find the same mysterious factor in the lives of the saints and servants of God; manifested the more clearly in proportion to their simplicity, surrender, and confidence of soul. How marvellously those lives develop! Francis, Teresa, Vincent de Paul, the Curé d'Ars—once they are given into the hand of God.

Now take another point. There are two sides to every vocation: unconditional giving of self to the call of God—"Here I am, send me!"—and the gift of power which rewards the total gift of self to God. In Christ's life we see these two movements in perfect balance. How humbly He submitted to the Will of the Father, totally absorbed in His business, and to the tests, pressure, suffering that came through circumstances; and yet how, though never in His own interest and never apart from His love and pity for man, there is always the Power to intervene, save, mould, defeat opposition, transform even the humble accidents of life. In all men and women of prayer deeply united to God that double state exists too. That handing of self over and the mysterious power that somehow acts through self in consequence—the right word said, the right prayer prayed. But only in proportion to the self-effacement. The power of course is God's, not ours. One hears people say, "He (or she) is simply wonderful!" Not at all! He or she

is the self-emptied channel of the only Wonderful—
the Mighty God, the Everlasting Father. When we
give ourselves to Him without reserve we become
points of insertion for the rescuing spirit of Love.
We are woven into the Redeeming Body so that we
may provide more and more channels for God. Think
of St. Francis with his special selfless love for lepers
and sinners; of St. Catherine of Siena saying, "I will
take your sins upon me"; of the Curé d'Ars, or Father
Wainwright of whom it was said, "You must be
either a drunkard or a criminal to know him well."
What were their lives really but this—channels for
the rescuing Spirit of Love?

*He entered into the ship with them and the wind
ceased, and there was a calm.*

Now are we able, because of our consecration and
self-oblivion, to enter a troubled situation with that
gift of peace and power? There is always something
of this in people whose lives are hidden in Christ.
"Father's bin to see 'im and so it's all right!" the
people of Dockland used to say when Father Wainwright had been at the death-bed of some apparently
heathen, degraded, unrepentant soul, pacifying by
his very presence.

So that deeply surrendered union with God and
docility to His requirements: that power of transforming circumstance, of exerting a pacifying, saving and compassionate action at our own cost, is an
essential part of the Pattern put before us.

Dwell on the two pictures included in this one
incident. Christ, "the Saint of Saints" as à Kempis
calls our Lord, snatching a few hours' solitude for that
communion with God which was the life of His life,
lifted for the time right away from all the struggles,
worries, perils, ceaseless demands of this life in which

He was normally immersed. And then His vision and knowledge of the poor little boat and its crew; He had left them to themselves and they were already in trouble, caught in a sudden storm on the lake. Surely it is in His instant response to that need, not in the wonder and joy of His mysterious prayer, that we are shown the full majesty and power of His holiness. That is a situation, contrast, test, demand, always turning up in the devout life—that call of those who need us taking us away from what we love to do. Do we meet it with exasperation or unwillingness, or with the power of a great compassion, united to the love of God? We are each one of us an instrument of His rescuing action; our lives as Christians are not complete without that, and His power will not be exerted through us except at considerable cost to ourselves. How gentle, humble, uncritical, full of zest we have got to be, if that power is to have a free path! Muzzy, "ca'-canny" Christianity is no good. A devotional life tainted by spiritual self-love or self-interest will never convey the saving power of God.

A self-oblivious, rescuing, helping love is the secret of intercession: a willingness to turn from our private communion with God and stretch out the hand of rescue, all the generous love of the redeeming spirit to those left hungry in the wilderness or caught in the storm. The minister of Christ must always be ready to do that, always be on guard against merely enjoying God.

It is love itself, Divine Love and not something abnormal and peculiar, which defeats circumstance and goes straight to the point, which rescues and re-assures. I love to think Christ had no special consciousness of performing an abnormal action, did not deliberately exert His superhuman power; that He was drawn across the stormy lake to the little boat in the tempest, as it were inevitably, by the single over-mastering impulse of His compassionate love. "Not drawn by necessity but drawn by charity," says à Kempis of the Incarnation and that principle runs right through the New Testament and makes ruth-less war in the name of Christ on the determinist and mechanist conceptions of life. Our Lord and His Saints transformed nature, almost without knowing it, in the strength of a great love.

Let us bring this element, this expression of the love of God, this passion for rescue, into relation with our life of prayer. See how in the last resort that difficult fluctuating life depends on His support and intervention; what a poor thin notion that is which regards prayer as something we do ourselves; some-thing which develops from state to state in a nice orderly way, according to a supernatural syllabus. We are labouring at the oars most of us, struggling against a head wind to keep our sense of direction. Natural surroundings and our own weaknesses are too much for us. We are helpless at the mercy of the storms of temptation, emotional distraction, doubt, worry, disillusionment, bereavement. They come down on us without warning and drive us off our course. And that is hard when we are known for Christians and supposed to be ready for everything that comes. When that happens all the calm beauty of the spiritual life seems a long way away. And it is just then above all other times that the miracle of prayer happens. Not always in a very sensational way. We do not always recognize at first who or what that steadying, peaceful pressure is that enters the little boat of the soul, pitching and tossing on the waves. But somehow the wind does cease and the reassuring pressure does come. He enters the ship and overrules the hurly-burly and sends peace.

Do you know that wonderful picture of our Lord's Descent into Hades which is called "The Harvest of Hell"?[1] It shows us the liberated soul of Christ passing straight from the anguish of the Passion to the delighted exercise of rescuing love. He comes with a sort of irresistible rush, bearing the banner of re-demption to the imprisoned spirits of those who knew Him not. There they are, pressing forward to the mouth of the cave, the darkness, narrowness, un-reality from which He comes to free them, free them at His own great cost. Nowhere, not even in the Resurrection garden, does He seem more victorious, more Divine. The awed delight of the souls He res-cues is nothing beside the rescuer's own ecstatic de-light. It is as if the soul released on Calvary could not wait a moment, but rushed straight to the awaitir ; joy of releasing the souls of other men. There is no hint of the agony and darkness through which He has won the power to do it. Everything is forgotten, the cost, the darkness, everything but the need which the Rescuer is able to meet. "Enter into the Joy of the Lord" means that among other things.

---

[1] Fra Angelico (San Marco, Florence).

VI

THE CROSS AND THE SACRAMENTS

WE have stood before four of our six windows now; four revelations of Reality, of the Radiance of -Eternal God poured through Christ on man. They are four manifestations of Absolute Love, four streams of generosity flowing from the Heart of Reality and entering and transforming the human world; giving New Life, Truth, Health, Rescue, always at the Giver's cost.

And now we pass from the effect to the act, to the state, the mystery on which all centres, from which all the effects flow; from the surface of existence, even spiritual existence, to its solemn and mysterious deeps. We stand, or kneel now, before the picture of a total self-abandonment, the uttermost expression of sacrificial love: the Cross.

And they were in the way going up to Jerusalem and Jesus was going before them and they were amazed and they that followed were afraid. (St. Mark x, 32.)

St. Luke says, "They understood none of these things." They understood not and were afraid to ask Him. There is something mysterious at the heart of man's life which becomes clear only, indeed can be endured only, with our surrender to God. Until then we do not understand and are afraid to ask. There is a suffering and a love twined so closely together that we cannot wrench them apart: if we try to, the love is maimed in the process, it loses its creative power and the suffering remains but without its aureole of willing sacrifice. Love makes the whole

79

difference between an execution and a martyrdom. Pain, and the willingness to risk pain, alone gives dignity and worth to human love and is the price of its creative power; without that, it is mere emotional enjoyment. It costs a lot to love any human being, even our nearest and dearest, to the bitter end. So God loved the world. And so too love and pain, tension, effort, loneliness, endurance, self-giving: these rule and condition all the victories of art and science and adventure. The Cross is the price of all real achievement. The Son of Man must suffer if He would fulfil all His possibilities. The crowning peace of the fully awakened, fully Christian soul is always that demand. To the outer eye the figure on the Cross who dominates this window may seem both lonely and idle—yet it is here, as St. Bonaventure said, that "great perfection is being taught to our souls."

"It is not the act of a good disciple," says St. John of the Cross, "to flee from the Cross in order to enjoy the sweetness of an easy piety." So here above all, by the Crucifix and what it means to us, we test the quality of our discipleship. What we think about the Cross means ultimately what we think about life, for "seek where you will," says à Kempis, "everywhere you will find the Cross." And when you have found it, what are you going to do about it? That is the question: look at it with horror or with adoration?

It has been said that the whole life of Christ was a Cross. I think that saying does grave injustice to its richness of response, to the real expansion and joy and beauty of His contacts with nature, children, friends; the true happiness we find again in the saints nearest to Him; the hours snatched for the deep joy of prayer and communion; the outburst of rejoicing when He discerns the Father's Will. But it was the deep happiness of the entirely self-abandoned, not the easy shallow satisfaction of those who live to express themselves and enjoy themselves; that Perfect Joy which St. Francis rediscovered in abjection; and which was ratified on La Verna when he was caught into the supernatural order and sealed with the wounds of Christ.

There is a marked contrast between the first phase of the Ministry with its confident movement within the natural world; mending what is wrong with it, using what is right in it and sharing the social life of men; and that after the Transfiguration, the second phase, with its sense of a deepening conflict with that easy, happy world; the conviction that what is deeply wrong with it can only be mended by sacrifice; that the Suffering Servant is the one who serves His brethren best. "Take up the Cross if you wish to follow Me!" The spiritually natural life is charming but it stops short of all that God asks of the really surrendered soul.

It was in the Passion, says St. John of the Cross, that Christ "finished that supreme work which His whole life, its miracles and works of power, had not accomplished: the union and reconciliation of human nature with the life of God." Here we learn all that it means to acknowledge Him as our Way, our Truth and our Life. I suppose no soul of any sensitiveness can live through Holy Week without an awed and grateful sense of being incorporated in a mystery of self-giving love which yet remains far beyond our span.

We saw how the first movement of Christ's soul was self-donation to the purpose of the Father, already stirring in His childish heart. "I must be about

F

my Father's business"—the one rule of His life and ours. It seems the most lovely of vocations at that point. The last movement of His soul was the utter self-giving of the Cross—

Into Thy hands . . . My God! My God! In this awful hour You seem a long way off. I seem forsaken. My whole soul is clouded by the dread mystery of pain and death. I thought there would be a victory, a rescue for your faithful child, and there is not. It looks almost as though You had forsaken me, as though my ultimate trust was betrayed. Yet even so I accept it. You and Your purposes matter, all is Yours, into Your hands I commend my spirit. . . .

That is the perfection of self-oblivious love. That is the true culmination of the story that began with the Baby at Bethlehem. It is a very lopsided revelation of God that gives us the manger without the Cross—those two windows stand north and south of the Altar where Christ gives Himself eternally to men. "We are made partakers of Christ," says the writer of the Epistle to the Hebrews; "if we hold the beginning of our confidence steadfastly to the end." The beginning is easy and lovely; it is the end that tests to the uttermost our courage and love. "Can you drink of My Cup and be baptized with My Baptism?" Not unless we care more about Him than about our own souls.

But there is the essence of the spiritual life. Profound submission to the mysterious Will of God declared in circumstance. And being what we are and the world what it is, that means for most of us Gethsemane and the Cross and the darkness of the Cross.

Lots of the saints have been through that. We don't begin to understand the Passion till we see what it was in their lives. For union with Christ means accepting the dread fact of human nature; that only those willing to accept suffering up to the limit are capable of giving love up to the limit; and that this is the kind of love which is the raw material of the redeeming life. Only those who place themselves in the hands of God without reserve and without fear are going to be used by Him to save. We want a lot of practice before we can manage this. It will not come out of an easy-going religion.

To look at the Crucifix—"the supreme symbol of our august religion"—and then to look at our own hearts; to test by the Cross the quality of our love— if we do that honestly and unflinchingly we don't need any other self-examination than that, any other judgment or purgation. The lash, the crown of thorns, the mockery, the stripping, the nails—life has equivalents of all these for us and God asks a love for Himself and His children which can accept and survive all that in the particular way in which it is offered to us. It is no use to talk in a large vague way about the love of God; *here* is its point of insertion in the world of men.

What about the dreadful moment when a great test of courage, great suffering, a great bereavement faced us and we knew we were for it and found the agony was more than we could face? The revelation that someone we trusted could not be trusted any more, that someone loved profit better than they loved us? How do we feel when we have to suffer for someone else's wrongdoing? How do we bear mockery and contempt, especially if it is directed at our religious life or at the unfortunate discrepancy between our religious life and our character? What about the sting, the lash, of humiliation or disappointment, the unfortunate events that stripped us of the seamless drapery of self-respect and convention and left us naked to the world; the wounds given by those we loved best; the loneliness inseparable from some phase of the spiritual life? All this happens over and over again. Can we weave it all into the sacrifice of love?

Here again Christ does not go outside our ordinary condition. He hallows real life. Can we hallow it? Can we bear to let the light of the window fall on our little fears, humiliations and pains and endure the chemical rays which can transform them into part of His sacrifice? Can we weave all that into the sacrifice of love, and what are we going to do with it if we can't? Our world is chaos without the Cross; for we never understand suffering until we have embraced it, turned it into sacrifice and given ourselves in it to God. After that we can say with the poet Claudel, "No more sin without God, no more crosses without Christ," and know that the Crucifix and the Eucharist are two aspects of one mystery.

I expect you remember Giotto's great fresco of the Crucifixion with Franciscan saints kneeling at the foot of the Cross, sharing their Founder's mysterious privilege. And then another, lovelier picture for which perhaps this gave the first suggestion, the fresco by Fra Angelico, in the Chapter House of San Marco at Florence, of the Founders of the Religious Orders adoring the Cross. The artist has spread out universally Giotto's conception beyond those whose special devotion is to the Crucifix and who have been visibly conformed to the Passion, and has brought together representatives of all men and women of

prayer of every type—indeed, all Christians of good
will. Here are St. Cosmas and St. Damian the good
physicians; holy women whose ministry was of the
most practical kind; the Magdalene full of penitence
and love—she supports the Blessed Virgin. Then we
see the great monastic founders, each with their particular vision and genius; teachers, scholars, those
who spread civilization or rescued from sin; and every
one linked with the Crucified, living in His aura,
working for His sake. They all carry through into
history by their own unlimited self-giving some frag-
ment of His love and life. That is the very heart of
religion; like an immense impetus of generosity, pouring out from the heart of Christ through His adoring
servants of every sort and kind on the world. It does
not matter much what their work is—the intellectual
labours of St. Jerome and St. Augustine; St. Bene-
dict's creation of the ordered life of obedience and
prayer and labour all subordinate to God; the fervour
of St. Francis; the absorbed gaze of Aquinas seeing
the key to that great mystery of being, to which he
had given his varied intellectual powers, bathed in
the Eternal Light.

Then we look up at the Crucifix from which all
these draw power and love; to Him to whom they
have given their lives and who gave them their man-
date, whose agents they are, the Saint of Saints.
And looking through the eyes of their adoring love
we see not torment and darkness, cruel physical pain
and its results, but the peace of a Divine and absolute
acceptance of selfless and abandoned love; so tranquil, so unstrained, so strangely full of joy—suffering
accepted and transfigured by the passion of redeeming love.

We are part of the Mystical Body of Christ. Can

we bear the light that falls from this window on our souls; the light that shows us what we were like in the moment when we were given the chance of sacrifice? Surely shame must overwhelm every one of us here. In the end we only triumph by that which we can endure and renounce. We do not begin to understand the Cross till we see what it has been in the lives of the saints.

Now take another point. There is a phrase which the Greek Liturgy is constantly applying to God in Christ—"O Lord and Lover of men." The whole religious movement of the drama of the Passion is gathered up in that. Re-enter that history and see what it means. In our meditation let us read and brood on the Gospel account of the Passion, all the curt notes crowded together. Detach them, take them separately, dwell upon them. The anointing by the woman of Bethany of One who never seemed more divine than now, accepting so peacefully the menacing web of events that begins to hem Him in. And even that gesture of love spoiled for Him by the sordid displeasure of His own disciples. All that stresses His isolation. And then the incredible beauty of that double manifestation of humble and generous service, the Last Supper and the Washing of the Feet, with their deep and selfless reverence and concern for our human weakness and need. And lastly, Gethsemane, the real crisis, the victory: nothing matters to Him after that. The first prayer of natural agony —If it is possible don't let this happen! I can't face it! And the second prayer—If I must go through with this, *Thy* Will be done! The spirit is willing— the flesh is weak. Because of that scene, at the very heart of human suffering we always find Christ, the

THE CROSS AND THE SACRAMENTS 87

Lord and Lover of men. We often feel we make such
a mess of our suffering: we seem to lose the essence
of the sacrifice because we can't face it; we beg to be
let off; we don't cut a heroic figure, don't stand up
to it. And so we think we have failed God. Gethsemane is the answer of the Divine Compassion to that
fear. After that He comes with a strange serenity to
the Betrayal and Peter's denial, His closest friend,
surely none the less hard to bear because foreseen.

Think of these events as they were, crowded together—"the dense and driven Passion" as Hopkins
called it. We often think we need a quiet time before
we make a great spiritual effort. Christ's quiet time
was Gethsemane and we know what that was like.
Think what each of these events meant, beating one
after another on a soul unique in its sensitiveness to
evil, sorrow, love—completely awake to its own awful
destiny and moving towards it in absolute loneliness
and still at every point pouring itself out in loving
care for men, self-given without hesitation to the
vocation of sacrifice because it was the Lord and
Lover of men; feeding and saving them ever since
by the fruits of His self-given love. For the Cross and
the Sacraments cannot be separated in the Christian's
thought of Christ. Only the utterly self-given is able
to give supernatural cleansing and supernatural food.

There is a type of ancient picture which shows all
the Sacraments centred in and dependent from the
Cross: the love self-given there giving itself for ever
to men, the undying source of grace and purification
and truth. It is a wonderful image of what the
Christian Church and Christian life really are, a con-
tinuation of the Incarnation. It reminds us that the
Spirit of Christ is now living and truly present with
and in His Church, His Family, His Mystic Body,

and, because of His one eternal sacrifice ever giving us His life, and that we are utterly and entirely dependent on that life as branches on the Vine, His touch still cleansing us, His hand still feeding us. Either secretly or sacramentally all living Christians are perpetual penitents and perpetual communicants, there is no other way of carrying on. The Eucharist represents a perpetual pouring out of His very life to feed and enhance our small and feeble lives. Think only of that as we kneel before the window of His Passion and a wonderful joy and gratitude tempers our shame.

Now turn and look at ourselves, our own lives, in the light of this revelation of the Charity of God. What courage, what humility, what absolute self-giving it requires of us if we are to be the channels through which that mysterious life is to be poured out on other men, and that is what it means to be Members of Christ. In Holy Communion we pledge ourselves to that—"the fellowship of His sufferings" . . . "In Thy presence is fullness of joy." Consider how drastically our idea of joy must be purified, how saturated with sacrificial love, before we can drink of the chalice of Christ. The Eucharist is the very heart of Christian worship because it is so rich and far-reaching in its significance; because it eludes thought, eludes emotion, relies on simple contact, humble and childlike receptiveness, sense quenching soul. It mixes together the extremes of mystery and homeliness; takes our common earthly experience of suffering, love, abandonment, death; and makes them inexpressibly holy and fruitful; takes the food of our natural life and transforms that into a channel of Divine Life.

How does our ordinary, homely, everyday life in

its spiritual detail harmonize with our Eucharistic practice? Does that consecration lie on the whole of it—family, work, social intercourse, friendship with the poor, intellectual adjustment and public duty, as well as on our secret correspondence with God? Is all that the material of a "reasonable, holy and living sacrifice"? How do our inward dispositions, our attitude to other people, harmonize with One who comes to us and gives us His very self for love?

The Christian's life is lived in the open, not in a pious cubby-hole. As Christ gives Himself to feed us, so we have to incarnate something of His all-loving, all-sacrificing soul. If we do not, then we have not really received Him. That is the plain truth. It has been said there are many ways and degrees of receiving the Blessed Sacrament. It really depends on how wide we open our hearts. A spiritually selfish communion is not a communion at all. "Let that mind be in us" which is actually offered to us at the Altar, because it was given to God's purpose on the Cross.

VII

THE GLORIFIED LIFE

WE have come to the end of our Retreat. What shall be the last window we look at, the last picture we take home? I think it should be the great east window which stands above the Altar—the Vision of Christ Triumphant in His Church, that is in all Christians, in *us*, in so far as we live up to the grandeur and beauty of our vocation and see what it really means to be members of Christ, children of God, inheritors of Heaven.

We are looking now at the crown, the fulfilment, the sanctification and meaning of our life with all its effort and mystery. What do we feel as we gaze at it? Surely cleansed, humbled, delighted. Window by window, the splendour of the Light of God has been shown to us in all its various degrees, in a Living Person. We see it within our own world in terms of our own humble experience, God manifest in the flesh, growing and changing yet always the same. All the different colours together make the Spectrum of Holiness.

And now we look up at perfect achievement, the Kingdom. Life in all its variousness expressing the perfect will and thought of God. And we realize that some part in that achievement, that perfection, is possible to us because its life consists in the triumphant light of Christ. From Him the grace and energy flows in which our Christian lives are lived. "In Thee and for Thee"—one without the other is no good. So all our feeble Godward thoughts and prayers, all the little acts and sufferings and renunciations and achievements in which His Spirit moves in us, all our tiny separate contributions that don't seem much by themselves, are part of this—Christ Triumphant in all His Christians; the fullness of the bit by bit revelation of reality incarnate among men, which we have tried to weave into our lives and must go on trying to weave into our lives. What a lovely picture to take back from our Retreat!

What we see is a generous uncalculated outpouring of life and light and love, so individual and yet so general that on one hand the relationship of each spirit to Christ is unique and complete as each soul touched by Him always feels it to be; and on the other hand, the love poured out on one subtracts nothing from the love given to all. We see in this great window Universal Life as the uttered thought of God—Angels and Archangels, Energies and Worlds —because all are centred on and inspired by the Word of God, the Wisdom of the Father—Divine Reason—Christ. We can't do away with the east window without throwing out of key the whole lighting of the Cathedral, for here we look into the heart of the light, life and love of which the other windows gave us expression and part.

That window really shows us the Church Triumphant as it exists in the thought of God if we could only see it. The Triumphant Church is not a collection of pious people with robes washed white— it is the whole of life's energy running right, sublimated and woven into the loving self-expression of God—it is the Kingdom of Heaven. Its frontiers must stretch till they embrace the whole Universe in its power, mystery and beauty and bring it under the rule of Christ, the intellectual radiance full of love.

For the work of the Incarnation, as St. Paul saw, is not finished till the whole of the created order is filled with God and, at the heart of the universe, ruling it in its most majestic sweep and its homeliest detail, we find His uttered Word, His love. That is the vision the east window gives us, pictured as best we can in a symbolic and partial way but, of course, in its wholeness quite beyond our conceiving. The great powers and dominations of the natural order and the penetrating Spirit of Wisdom which, out of the heart of creation, gazes on God and the seraphic Spirit of Love that adores Him,

> *Angels and Archangels, Cherubim and Seraphim continually do cry*
> *Holy, Holy, Holy; Lord God of Sabaoth,*
> *Heaven and Earth are full of the Majesty of Thy Glory. . . .*

And you and I are committed, as baptized Christians, to what has been given His deep and touching earthly revelation, to the steady loyal effort, in our own small place and way, towards bringing that mounting vision a little nearer completeness, bringing a little more of that Kingdom in. Each faithful upward glance, each movement of trust, each act of selfless love, helps it on. A time such as we have had here is only justified if it brings that mounting vision into focus again; reminds us of what it means to be Inheritors of Heaven. The Hallowing of the whole Universe, physical, mental and spiritual in all its grades, the infinitely great and the infinitely small, giving our lives at whatever cost to the helping of the fulfilment of their sacramental promise—we must take sides in some way for that, because we are the Children of God.

Those thoughts kill all self-occupied fuss. They brace and delight us, remind us that our religion is not a refuge from Reality, it is a demand that we face Reality with all its difficulties, opportunities, implications; that we face God and His whole mysterious purpose and our own solemn responsibility to Him.

When Christ said, "My Father and your Father, My God and your God," He said it, not in the easy way we repeat what we think a consoling text. *Is* it consoling? Is it not tremendous, searching? Does it not ask for a tremendous response? We know what His own response was like and what it entailed. Was He not making a declaration which must transfigure the whole lives of those who realize all that is implied in it? Sweeping them into a closer union with His vision and joy and sufferings? Conferring on them the tremendous privilege of partnership? Fellow-workers with God because co-heirs with Christ. Do let us take that literally! "Christ," says de Caussade, "calls us *all* to perfection because He calls us all to submit to the Will of the Father and this is the same thing as Perfection." It is the complete acceptance of our life as Children of God, part of His creative purpose; it is "being made the Children of God and of the Light" as the baptismal service has it.

Look at the east window and see the vocation to which we are called, a vocation which makes us in the most actual sense members of His Body, that is, part of a spiritual organism filled with the Spirit of God, fed and energized by His life and each one committed to carrying out some share in His work. For all the marvellous and varied energy of mind and body can be part of His Triumph and serve His end —all are perfected by subjection to Christ the King.

This is what St. John Eudes means by his startling saying, "A Christian soul living in grace is part of Christ Himself"—not only by a pious life but by living in the energy of God. Holding that sentence in our minds, let us turn round and look again at the windows which light the soul's cathedral; at what they reveal and what they demand, if we are to be part of Christ Himself and so partners in His Mystery.

"My Father and your Father" means that we are children of the Eternal Perfect, of the supernatural world. The vision of the east window in all its splendid variousness is a vision of our home life— all things restored in Christ—the Kingdom of God. There it is in all its eternal power and beauty. And here all round are the homely labours, self-givings and sufferings through and in which it is to be manifested among men, but always in direct dependence on the unseen Splendour of God. That means an act of prayer at the heart of every act of service—a self-offering to His purpose so that the action may be His and not our own. That, in its perfection, is the secret of the saints. *I live—yet not I!* Christ is the boundless source of energy and love. Our petty little worries, rebellions, faults, animosities fade and shrivel when we see our total destiny like that and sink our small affairs in the vast tide of the Spirit's life.

Do you remember how in St. Patrick's *Confession* he tells how one night he *saw* Christ, praying in him and above him; and he was overwhelmed with awe, considering who prayed within him and a voice said, "I am the Spirit who prays in thee." So it has always been with the saints, channels of the Spirit, and so it may be with us, if we too give ourselves without

reserve: willing to face the suffering and conflict which are the fruit not merely of our own meanness but of the world's evil and which become our privilege if we give ourselves to the increase of the triumph of Christ.

So here we stand at the end of our Retreat and ask, "How, so far, has my heart, soul, mind, strength, my secret prayer and outer service played its part as a unit of the Body of Christ? What has it done to further His teaching, healing, rescuing, sacrificial work? How have my God-given energies contributed to the purposes of God?"

None of us can hope to do much in *all* these departments; some are called to one, some to another. Not all are teachers, not all can pour out that living and beautiful compassion which heals the wounds of life; not all are allowed to be with Christ on the Cross. But we each have our place and job in His economy; it is a triumph of balanced energy and deep peace.

Does the light of the window illuminate my special powers and opportunities? Perhaps they may lie specially in one of these departments, or perhaps in a humble, supple, self-giving life which keeps open in prayer the channel of love and finds place for something of each. Christ's Spirit, if I let it, can act through mine—praying in me and above me as St. Patrick said—and I was given to Him in baptism and gave myself to Him again of my own free will *for* this purpose, to be one more transmitter of God's power and love.

From the very first the transmitters have been ordinary, faulty people like us. "He gave Himself in either kind"—not to a collection of saints but to unstable Peter, dubious Thomas, pushful James and John. But they were surrendered and so could be

used in His triumph, woven into the tissue of the
Church that transmits His loving, saving, triumphant, all-sacrificing Love.

Well! what have we done about all this? "He is
in the world and the world knows Him not"—
largely because His members fail to disclose Him;
because those who should be the channels of the outpouring spirit of Charity block its passage by hardness, selfishness, apathy, love of spiritual comfort, a
petty and sterile religious outlook; too frightened to
lose their lives and give themselves with undemand-
ing generosity in order to find the all-generous life of
God. The east window and the Altar go together.
With them is the secret of life.

Lots of people love the great inspiring vision of
the window, the beauty and splendour of God: they
feel able to worship that; it fills them with exaltation
and awe. But the plain, homely Altar that stands
underneath it, where bread must be broken and the
cup poured out and which is our strange answer to
the revelation of the Glory of God, an answer first
made in our name by Christ, our High Priest—they
cannot do with that. Again and again they draw
near and wish to join the Angels and Archangels; but
first there is something they have got to leave on the
Altar—their mite, their food, their oblation, their
self-interest, self-love, self-will. "Absolute self-giving," says St. John of the Cross, "is the only path
from the human to the Divine."

We are mysterious little creatures, and we do not
understand ourselves. We feel very tiny as we stand
on the vast Cathedral floor and see the great pillars
rising all around us to the dim vault; and the windows with their pictures of a perfect holiness and love
are all the more daunting because they show that

holiness and love within the arena of our own lives, so far beyond us and yet so divinely near, emerging in utmost humbleness right down in the common life of men.

But as our pilgrimage proceeds, as we get used to the Cathedral light, we feel something comes through the windows that is strangely akin to us, that streams down into our souls and there awakes a first response —the light of the world to show us Reality, the *Lumen Christi.*

Have you ever seen the Easter Eve ancient ceremony when the Light of Christ is brought into the church? a taper wreathed in spring flowers, brought in from outside, the Light of the great world brought in to light the sanctuary lamp. How significant that is! And it is in fostering, strengthening, steadying the response to that Light that we fulfil our true meaning, become more real in the sight of God and make our tiny contribution to the Triumph of Life. For in the deepest sense, even that response is not truly our own. It is God Incarnate, God in His deep humanity, the Spirit proceeding from the Father and the Son, indwelling His little creatures, who stirs in us and initiates our new life towards Him—a life, as Brunner says, which "puts an end to our falsehood and our solitude." Think of these words; they reach to the root of our unrest.

And now we begin to see a certain sequence in the Mystery through which that life is revealed to us; a life born in such lowliness in a stable among the animals, right down in the natural life and developing among homely things: developing quite slowly, without sensational incident, subject to all the homely tests, strains, joys and duties of our human existence; and through and in them increasing in wisdom and

G

stature: confronted in the wilderness with life's crucial choice and rejecting everything less than God, everything that ministers to self-will. And so emerging into the light of truth and able to manifest truth, teaching the Will of God for men and the path men must follow to God.

And because truth has been revealed to life, there is born in it that wide and loving and creative compassion which is the only source of healing and help. And by the interplay of that pure truth and that warm compassion, life becomes filled with a rescuing and redeeming Power which transcends difficulties and does not notice labours; and that Power is made perfect in Sacrifice—the Eucharist, Gethsemane, the Cross.

And thus we are led up to Christ glorified, revealed at last as the very meaning of the Universe, and down to His ceaseless self-giving in those gifts and graces of the life of prayer and communion in which His very life is constantly offered to us. Offered, not merely for our own consolation or improvement, but as the life of the Body, binding us and Him together in the bonds of love to form together that true, invisible Church of which no man knows the boundaries but God alone and which is the eternal living instrument of the Father's Will—a reasonable, holy, living sacrifice.

Abide in Me and I in you; continue ye in My love. . . .

And when He had showed Himself to them and they had learned this, the disciples went away to their own homes.

POINTS FOR MEDITATION

[It was Evelyn Underhill's practice to present her retreatants with suggestions for private meditation during their retreat. The following list accompanied her addresses on the Light of Christ.]

THE Revelation of God is not a book or a doctrine but a living Person.

EMIL BRUNNER.

We shall never learn to know ourselves except by endeavouring to know God, for beholding His greatness, we realize our littleness, His purity shows our foulness, and by meditating on His humility we find how very far we are from being humble.

ST. TERESA.

However high be your endeavours, unless you renounce and subjugate your own will—unless you forget yourself and all that pertains to yourself—not one step will you advance on the road to perfection.

ST. JOHN OF THE CROSS.

The truth is that the only key to the Christian life is the life of Christ: That the only solution to the many problems that thicken round our lives as we live them is to be found in the study of His life as He lived it; and that we shall never begin to understand what we ourselves are until we begin to understand what He is.

R. H. J. STEUART.

It is not in the gifts He received but in the virtues He practised that Christ is our model. That which is asked of you, so that you may resemble Him, is to make the same use as He did of the gifts of God, according to the measure in which you have received them.

J. N. GROU.

The mystery revealed, in a unique degree and form, in Christ's life, is really a universal spiritual-human law; the law of suffering and sacrifice, as the one way to joy and possession, which has existed, though veiled till now, since the foundation of the world.

F. VON HÜGEL.

PRAYER

Teach us, O Lord, to do little things as though they were great, because of the majesty of Christ who does them in us and who lives our life; and to do the greatest things as though they were little and easy, because of His omnipotence.

PASCAL.

THE NEED OF RETREAT[1]

A FIRST retreatant lately told me that when she confessed to her husband what she intended to do, he took his pipe from his mouth and said earnestly: "Go, my dear. Go, by all means! You're just about due for a spot of re-birth." That man, it seems to me, had a very clear idea of one function of a retreat: its power of causing the re-birth of our spiritual sense, quickening that which has grown dull and dead in us, calling it out into light and air, giving it another chance.

Most of us are bitterly conscious of the extent in which we are at the mercy of our surroundings: which grow ever more and more insistent in their pressure, their demands on our attention and time; less and less suggestive of reality, of God. They call out and keep out the least spiritual side of our nature: and almost insensibly, often with the very best intentions, and under plea of good works, family duties, social obligations, we capitulate to the surface activities of existence, the ceaseless chain of passing events. We forget that awestruck upward glance which is the mark of the spiritual man. Then we lose all sense of proportion; become fussy, restless, full of things that simply must be done, quite oblivious of the only reason why anything should be done. Our prayers become more and more like supernatural shopping lists, less and less like that conversation between one friend and another which is the ideal of Thomas à Kempis. We can't rest in the Lord; there really

[1] Address given by Evelyn Underhill at the Annual Meeting of the Association for Promoting Retreats. *The Vision*, Jan., 1932.

isn't time for that. Besides, there's the telephone, which may be trusted to ring at the most shattering moment. So we gradually forget what interior silence is like, and seldom enter the interior world: and the result of this is appreciated only too well by all those with whom we have to deal. When we have reached this stage, nothing is going to save us but that Spot of Re-birth. We need a re-quickening of the spark of the soul; a re-emergence of the 'fine point of the spirit'—that most sacred and least considered element of human personality, so easily shoved down into the cellar, smothered and forgotten in the pressure of practical everyday life.

That might be called the clinical reason for retreats. Now take another reason. Our so-called civilization gets more and more complicated, more and more noisy. It is like one of those mills where the noise of the looms makes it impossible for the workers to hear each other speak. And if we go on at it long enough without a break we begin to think the looms are all that matter, and we are merely there to keep them going and must not bother about anything else. In other words, I am sure there is a real danger that Christian spirituality in its deepest and loveliest reaches will be killed out by the pressure and ·demands of the social machine, and even of the ecclesiastical machine. Man will get ever more utilitarian and this-world, and will wholly forget his true relation to God. I am sure you remember the beautiful letter of Baron von Hügel, in which he tells his pupil how all that we do has a double relatedness. It is part of the chain of cause and effect which makes up human life; and also it is, or can be, joined directly to God, the Changeless Reality who gives meaning to that life. To realize, make, keep up that double connection—this is to be fully human, fully alive; and how are we to teach and establish that in the scutter of the modern world? Even religion tends to become more and more pragmatic, utilitarian; more and more active, and less and less inward; more and more of a chain of doings, less and less of an attachment, a being.. And so by a curious paradox, as man's physical universe gets larger, his true horizon shrinks. He has become the slave of the clattering loom. He can't hear his own soul speak.

Now those who control the modern factory—wiser in their generation than the children of light—know what all this means in the exhausting and impoverishing of human material, in nervous tension, apathy, unrest. So there is no good factory without its welfare department, its rest room, its opportunity for quiet. To withdraw the worker at times from the clatter and pressure is to increase the quantity and quality of the work. So I sometimes think retreats should be regarded as a bit of spiritual welfare work; quite essential to the organization of the Church, and specially to the efficiency of its ministers. I am sure that were the making of at least a yearly retreat an absolute obligation of the priesthood, this would be a far more direct Way of Renewal than some of those now proposed.

I don't mean by this to recommend the retreat for merely practical reasons—because it makes the effective active Christian even more active and effective than before. I would rather recommend it because it puts in the foreground and keeps in the foreground that which is, after all, the first interest of religion— so easily lost sight of—the one thing needful—the soul's relation to God. That relation is so subtle, so invisible, so deeply personal, and yet so powerful—

how is its delicate beauty to be savoured, and its
humbling influence felt, while Martha runs from the
gas-stove to the scullery, listening with one ear to the
loud-speaker declaiming morning prayers? We need
for that such a silence and leisure as we get in a good
retreat; what one of the mystics called a "rest most
busy." Then the repressed elements of our truest
being can emerge and get light and air; and perhaps
such a renewal of faith, hope and charity—those three
virtues that are trained wholly towards God—that
they may keep their heads above water, when re-
immersed in the torrent of the world. And here I
venture to say that it seems to me that in the special
circumstances and needs of the Christian life in our
day we make a very grave mistake if we identify too
closely the ordinary retreat with the Ignatian form.
Certainly there are souls who can use the Ignatian
form again and again with sincerity and profit. Their
temperature-chart runs an uneven course. They need
again and again to be reminded of first principles, to
be trued-up to the pattern, and make in one way or
another the crucial choice between the Two Stan-
dards. But we are beginning to realize that St.
Ignatius never meant his masterpiece to be turned
into a yearly exercise for the devout. It is too powerful, searching, even shattering, for that. I believe the
retreat as a part of our normal spiritual routine will
yield on the whole its fullest results when we regard
it more often and more generally, in Abbot Delatte's
beautiful phrase, as an opportunity of "steeping our
souls in the beauty of the mysterious." To dwell
quietly and without self-occupation in the atmosphere of God is surely the best of all ways of re-
dressing the balance between the temporal and
eternal sides of our life. It is this aspect of the retreat

experience which seems to me to deepen, steady and enrich personality; it is this which produces the "Spot of Re-birth," and sends the retreatant back to the world more able to find the inward in the outward than before. In relation to this aspect, and the production of this atmosphere, the conductor has a special responsibility; for nothing that he does here will be of the slightest use to his retreatants, unless it proceeds from his own interior life with God.

And finally, what is to be the real objective—the aim—which we who believe in the retreat movement set before ourselves? We have said that it shall not be merely practical or merely remedial. It must include and look beyond both those aims. The object is the same as the object of the Christian life— sanctity—the production, fostering and maintenance of holiness. To sanctify, as Von Hügel was fond of saying, is the biggest thing out. Now souls are sanctified by the pressure and cleansing action of the Spirit, acting through and in the events of everyday life. But in order that the action of the Spirit may produce this effect, we know that a particular disposition, outlook, temper, is also required in the soul. And how is that to be produced? Perhaps most easily and directly by taking the soul from its normal preoccupations and placing it in an atmosphere and condition in which, with the minimum of distraction, it can attend to and realize God. And this in essence is a retreat.

Isn't it worth while to make some effort to create and keep going houses in which so great a thing can be done? Our increased capitulation to pace and noise makes it more and more necessary to provide such opportunities for realizing our spiritual status, and learning the width of the chasm which separates deep from distracted prayer. It is not easy under everyday conditions to learn and maintain the art of steadfast attention to God; yet no art could more certainly serve His purposes than this. "One loving spirit sets another on fire." The Church will win the world for Christ when—and when only—she works through living spirits steeped in prayer.